SUCCESSFULLY MARKETING CLINICAL TRIAL RESULTS

WHAT DO THE EXPERTS SAY ABOUT THE BOOK?

Pharmaceutical Companies

"An illuminating look at the dos and don'ts of effectively communicating clinical trial results."

Ian Talmage. Ian has held senior positions in global marketing in major pharmaceutical companies based in the **UK**, **US**, **Sweden**, **Switzerland**, **The Netherlands** and **Germany**

"Weaving together all the threads in a seamless how-to guide for pharmaceutical product managers."

David Spencer, Ph.D., Chief Operating Officer
Biolex Inc., Pittsboro, North Carolina, **USA**

Professional Service Firms

"Delivers the essentials for success in medical marketing."

Alain Rusterholtz, Director
Conseil d'Entreprises, Paris, **France**

"Shows how to increase the value of the brand and maximise return on investment."

Mike Gibbs, Chief Executive Officer
Sherborne Gibbs Limited, Birmingham, **UK**

Media for the Healthcare Industry

"Excellent reading, based on very good research. Has the potential to become a reference book for marketers."

Andreas Guhl, MD, Ph.D, Editor
Health & Sales

"Great real-world examples, very useful to any marketer."

Peter Stegmaier, Editor
Pharma Relations

SUCCESSFULLY MARKETING CLINICAL TRIAL RESULTS

Winning in the Healthcare Business

DR GÜNTER UMBACH

GOWER

Published by
Gower Publishing Limited
Gower House
Croft Road
Aldershot
Hampshire
GU11 3HR
England

Gower Publishing Company
Suite 420
101 Cherry Street
Burlington
VT 05401-4405
USA

British Library Cataloguing in Publication Data
Umbach, Gunter
  Successfully marketing clinical trial results : winning in
  the healthcare business
  1.Drugs – Marketing 2.Drugs – Testing
  I.Title
  615.1'0688

  ISBN-10: 0 566 08643 3
  ISBN-13: 978-0-566-08643-4

Library of Congress Control Number: 2006931606

Printed and bound in Great Britain by Antony Rowe Ltd, Chippenham, Wiltshire

CONTENTS

Section 20: Implementing the Project   177

Section 21: Becoming a Project Leader   185

ACKNOWLEDGEMENTS

I would like to acknowledge the following people who offered valuable personal contributions or organized seminars with me:

Alain Rusterholtz (Paris, France)

Michael Gibbs (Birmingham, UK)

Dr. Michaela Gottwald (Heidelberg, Germany)

Mónica García Sánchez (Madrid, Spain)

Karolina Kozlicka (Warsaw, Poland)

Bojana Kržič, MD, MSc (Ljubljana, Slovenia)

Sarah Spanswick (London, UK)

I also thank the participants of my workshops and the marketing professionals of my personal coaching sessions.

Special thanks to Jonathan Norman, Publisher and Gillian Riley, Senior Desk Editor at Gower, UK and to Gerlinde van Kerkom and Katrin zur Nieden, MediSign, Cologne, Germany for their artwork and illustrations

Comments or questions are welcome: contact the author at www.umbachpartner.com

TO THE READER

Dear Reader,

This book has a power that will not be experienced if it is merely read.

It will take you only a few minutes to read each of the sections. Choose the tips, suggestions and recommendations that seem appropriate to you and action them.

What may seem a simple idea when first read, could prove to be a gateway to personal success once started.

Let this book inspire you.

Kind regards,

Günter Umbach

Dr. Günter Umbach

CODES OF PRACTICE

Transparency

Full transparency and accountability requires that the complete trial results be made available to the public without any bias or selectivity in reporting. Not reporting the results of negative trials is ethically and scientifically unacceptable.

Pharmaceutical companies should endorse good publication practice guidelines.

The industry should promote adherence to these guidelines.

Standards

The process from publishing of a protocol for a planned study to reporting the results of study must be done to exacting standards. All ethical and legal standards need to be applied in all communications – whatever the medium. All communications must ensure a fair balance and must adhere to the relevant Codes of Practice in company, industry and country. For examples please see those put forth by the following organizations.

Selected relevant organizations

- International Federation of Pharmaceutical Manufacturers and Associations (IFPMA): www.ifpma.org
- European Federation of Pharmaceutical Industries and Associations (EFPIA): www.efpia.org
- Japanese Pharmaceutical Manufacturers Association (JPMA): www.jpma.or.jp/english
- Pharmaceutical Research and Manufacturers of America (PhRMA): www.phrma.org
- Association of the British Pharmaceutical Industry (ABPI): www.abpi.org.uk
- Verband Forschender Arzneimittelhersteller (VFA): www.vfa.de
- US Food and Drug Administration (FDA): www.fda.gov
- Medical Research Council (MRC): www.mrc.ac.uk
- World Health Organization (WHO): www.who.int

Please check their websites for details.

Benefits

This book explains the do's and don'ts of communicating clinical trial results so that everybody can win: patients, physicians, payors, pharmaceutical companies and other parties involved such as hospitals and professional organizations.

INTRODUCTION

Personal story

Some managers believe in long-term, theory-driven, central-office strategic plans.
Their credo: if you get the strategy right, the rest will follow automatically. However, as I
have learned through experience, this is not the case. When as marketing manager I was
given the job of marketing the clinical trial results of a major brand, I initially developed
a neat marketing strategy and sent it to stakeholders. Do you know what happened?
Absolutely nothing!

Designed for your career

This book has been written for you from the perspective of how to support your
professional performance and strengthen your personal success in a tough business
environment. The participants of my seminars and workshops have also contributed
through their questions, comments, objections and suggestions.

The blueprint for your success

The recipe for success? First, get the strategy right. Then move from theory to practice.
Start with the conceptual approach and then execute the project. Ensure that your
strategy actually gets implemented. Make things happen. Act.

Examples and case studies as illustrations

I will often use a fictional substance, which I will call 'Substantin', and a fictional brand named 'Examplex' in my examples and case studies, which are based on real-life cases. This book gives recommendations and tips, but no concrete rules. You may choose what is suitable for you from the range of suggestions offered. Pick what is appropriate and adapt the recommendations to your individual situation. The book does not address legal questions, however, so please check the legal requirements and regulations in your own country.

PERSONAL GOALS AND OBJECTIVES

Imagine your goals

Your Goals and Objectives

 Successfully Marketing
Clinical Trial Results

How do you define success?

What are your performance indicators?

What objectives do you want to achieve?

Imagine yourself crossing the finish line; what do you want to have accomplished? What do you want to have achieved? You may want to ask yourself the following questions before beginning the project:

- which objectives do I want to achieve when marketing clinical trial results?
- how will I know that I have done an excellent job?
- what are my key performance indicators?

Define your success criteria

Success Criteria in Marketing

Win in the market

Sales

Prescriptions

Market share

Revenue

The success criteria for marketers are usually straightforward:

- number of prescriptions
- market share
- revenue
- profit
- return on investment.

Identify success criteria for the clinical development team

Success Criteria in 'Medical'
Papers in prestigious conferences
Publications in renowned journals
Hot topic for opinion leaders
High awareness among doctors
Enhanced reputation

People in medical and clinical development departments have their own objectives. For them the reputation and prestige of their clinical trial programme is of great importance. Success from their perspective is represented by:

- presentations in the main sessions of international congresses
- highly visible publications in peer-reviewed journals
- the trial and its results becoming a hot topic for opinion leaders
- increased awareness among doctors.

The experienced marketer understands the difference in objectives between clinical development and marketing, and considers the above objectives as stepping stones on the way to more sales.

Get everything on the table

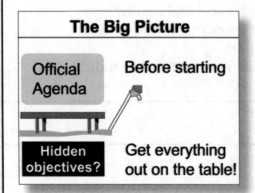

In most companies, there are overt (obvious) and covert (hidden) objectives. The latter are usually associated with power plays and personal career plans. Examples of covert rules include: 'Pleasing the boss is more important than pleasing the customer', 'Always keep your turf clean', 'Change jobs frequently'. Make sure you are aware of these hidden rules before you assume responsibility for the project.

Your project is only a piece in the overall company picture. Find out if there is a secret agenda behind the project. Understand the tensions between the various functions. Get everything out on the table. Ask your boss explicitly about it.

Your aim is to avoid embarking on an impossible mission or ending up as scapegoat or martyr in your organization.

Seize your opportunities

The Business Opportunity

A clinical trial
is a gift to your
marketing people

Unfortunately, some of them
will not even unwrap it.

A clinical trial is your opportunity to get a bigger slice of the global pharmaceutical market which is valued at approximately €360 000 million. Even though the world has become a tougher place to do pharmaceutical business, several forecasts expect the market to show solid single-digit growth in the years to come.

Pharmaceutical companies spend vast sums of money conducting high-quality clinical trials. In the USA, they spend approximately $7 000 million on trials. Unfortunately, the results of many trials never emerge from the shadows.

Clinical studies offer an abundance of marketing opportunities. The tragedy is that many companies do not realize the options they provide. The sad truth is they sit at the 'banquet' of their research results and never help themselves from the plate. They fail to market their trials effectively. Remember, a study not marketed is a study not done. In addition, a clinical trial is a great personal opportunity for you to learn and to grow.

ANALYZING THE MARKET AND DEVISING A STRATEGY

Design a winning strategy

Developing the Strategy

| Content | Message | What |

Modes of expression

Communication activities

} How

| Target groups | | To whom |

What is the thinking behind your strategy? Try the following conceptual approach.

- *Content*: review the wealth of raw results based on the scientific data and develop the concept of your message (what).
- *Modes of expression*: find the proper modes of conveying your message, which means selecting appropriate words, style, layout, diagrams and images (how).
- *Communication activities*: transfer your message through communication channels (how).
- *Target groups*: your message reaches its destination, in other words the customers you selected (to whom).

You should also consider the where and when of your communication. There is no one-size-fits-all approach to developing your strategy. You need to tailor the strategy and the individual marketing activities to the needs and wants of your customers.

Get to know your market

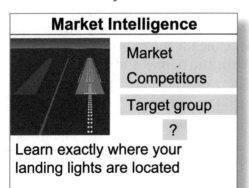

Market Intelligence

Market

Competitors

Target group

?

Learn exactly where your landing lights are located

Examine and investigate your market so you have crystal-clear answers to the following questions:

- what is your market segment?
- who are your competitors?
- what is your target group and who are your main customers?

On the basis of having analysed the past, develop a sixth sense for future market trends. Ask yourself: what's coming next? and try to anticipate market changes.

Identify and study your target groups

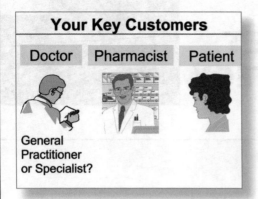

Think customer needs right from the start! Never lose sight of your customers.

Ask yourself: who are the main decision makers among my customers?

Who has the greatest influence on making the business transaction?

The key decision makers in patented prescription drugs are the prescribing physicians. It is their perception of how much value your product and your company will add which will determine the success or failure of your marketing efforts.

Take the time to clarify the roles of the pharmacist, of patient advocacy groups, of reimbursement authorities and of other stakeholders in the decision making process. What percentage of your budget do you want to allocate to each of these groups?

Apply the Pareto Principle

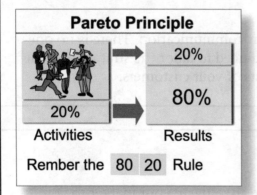

When planning the resources you want to direct towards the various groups, remember the 'Pareto Principle'. This concept implies that 20 per cent of the activities produce 80 per cent of the outcome whereas 80 per cent of activities produce only 20 per cent of the outcome. Inappropriately applied effort will divert precious resources and represent a dispersion of energy.

Set clear priorities. Focus on your key customers who are responsible for the majority of the sales.

For example, do you have a list from your sales force with the names and addresses of the doctors who are the main prescribers of your product? Consider talking to an agency specialising in customer relationship management to get fresh ideas.

Find out what doctors want

Understand your customers' mindset. Ask yourself: does my planned approach coincide with customer needs? Market research has shown that doctors' interest in study results is very limited, sometimes close to zero. Face the fact that basically they are not interested in your study results.

Your customers – like everyone else – seek their own self-interest. The doctor's concern remains: What is the benefit for me and my patients? You need to ask yourself:

- what customer problem do you solve from the perspectives of the doctors and their patients?
- how are your product and the associated trial results useful?
- why are they important?

To make sure that you are on the right track, you may want to discuss your thoughts with one or two trusted doctors.

Use evidence to shape perception

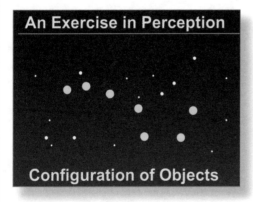

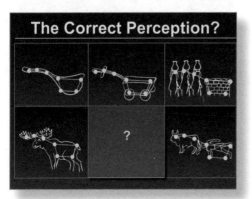

What role does perception play? Customer perception is extremely important, since it is this perception that determines the customer's behaviour. Remember: marketing is *not* a battle of products, it is a battle of perceptions.

Consider the following. The constellations of stars are considered by different cultures to resemble various characters, animals or objects. The choice of meaning varies according to the observer and where they come from. You may know the constellation of seven stars near the North Pole star.

In the US most people call this constellation the 'Big Dipper', in the UK it is called 'The Plough' and in other parts of Europe 'The Wagon'. In other countries around the world it is also known by a variety of different names.

We 'see' a different shape and use a different name depending on what we have learnt or where we have been brought up.

Which image do you want to create?

The Right Impression

What perception do you want to encourage?

What impression do you want to create?

What image do you wish to convey?

You cannot alter the data. You cannot change the trial results. You can, however, address the following questions:

- what kind of perception do you want to encourage?
- what impression do you want to convey?
- what picture do you want to paint?

Remember that the results must support whatever you communicate.

DEVELOPING YOUR CONTENT

Study the scientific results

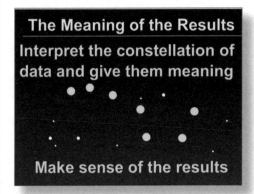

The Trial Results

Research Report

Inspect

Examine

Scrutinize

A clinical trial yields a wealth of research results. There are usually primary and secondary parameters. Do your homework and inspect the scientific results thoroughly. Review them carefully. You may have to dig deeply. Enlist the support of colleagues from the clinical development or the medical marketing department, or of an outside consultant, to help you.

Interpret the data

The Meaning of the Results

Interpret the constellation of data and give them meaning

Make sense of the results

Give meaning to the results by answering the following questions:

- what does the data mean to the doctor?
- how do you interpret the results so that they are relevant to the doctor?
- which conclusions can you draw for the practice of medicine?

This task takes a razor-sharp mind, time and commitment. Do *not* expect your advertising agency to do this for you – they usually lack both the medical expertise and the research background.

Develop your message

From Results to Message

Results: The set of numbers, tables, diagrams and charts

Give meaning

The Message:
What you want to convey
to your customers

Based on the trial results and the meaning you attribute to the scientific findings, develop answers for the following questions:

- what is your core message?
- what do you want to communicate?
- what is your story?

Take the time to think.

Ensure that your message is based on scientific evidence.

Positive Result: Message

Scientific result

Patient message

HIV test is positive ...

You've got the HIV virus

An HIV (human immunodeficiency virus) test usually shows either a positive or a negative test result. A *positive* test result is bad news for the patient (who has been infected with a deadly virus). A positive result implies the following message to the patient: 'You are infected with HIV'.

Negative Result: Message

Scientific result

Patient message

HIV test is negative ...

Everything is fine

A *negative* HIV test result usually means that the patient has not developed antibodies against the human immunodeficiency virus: positive and encouraging news for the patient. The underlying message is: 'Everything is fine'. However, a poorly developed and communicated message can have devastating consequences. In the past, patients told that 'Your HIV test is negative' have misinterpreted the statement as meaning 'You have the disease'.

Avoid irrelevant messages

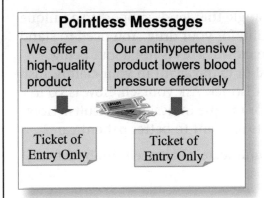

One company for which I undertook consultancy work considered promoting their new product as a 'high-quality' product. However, most products on the market were considered 'high-quality' products. Hence this is a marketing approach that does not communicate any competitive advantage. We therefore changed the message.

A second company marketed their new blood-pressure-lowering drug as 'effectively reducing blood pressure'. Yet this is exactly what you would expect of all blood-pressure-lowering drugs. Once again, this approach does not communicate any competitive advantage.

Look for competitive advantages

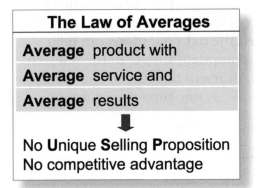

The market is flooded with competing products using similar messages. Are the characteristics of your product, your service and your trial results different from those of your competitors? Does your message convey a competitive advantage?

Work the angles considering all data

Unique Selling Point

Ask: How is the trial unique?

In what way is the trial special?

What distinguishes the trial from all other trials?

How are the results distinctive?

Look for an angle that lends support to a unique or special claim for your drug. You need to stand out from the crowd. This is not about being experimental or extravagant in your claims, just about being distinct. Ask yourself: how is your trial special or unique in design or results? How are the results relevant to better patient care?

Always communicate a balanced risk-benefit ratio.

Ask the right questions

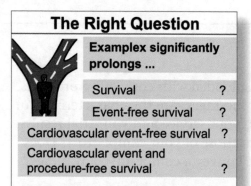

The Right Question

Examplex significantly prolongs ...

Survival	?
Event-free survival	?
Cardiovascular event-free survival	?
Cardiovascular event and procedure-free survival	?

There are often nuggets of information you can extract from the wealth of research results. Information needs to be both clinically relevant and helpful in distinguishing your product by supporting a competitive advantage. Sometimes asking yourself the right questions can help identify the appropriate answer in the research data. Probe in different directions. The example shows how you can fine-tune your questions.

Seek insights from the investigators

The Investigators

An immense knowledge base

Discuss questions with clinical investigators

Gain insights from the experts

The clinical researchers who undertook the trial form a huge knowledge base. Talk to them. Ask your medical colleague to introduce you. You will usually be given a warm welcome. Make time for a chat with them. What were their experiences of the trial? What impressions and ideas can they offer?

Set the right focus

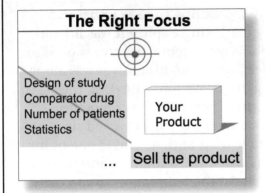

You need to emphasize the benefits of the product and not the characteristics of the trial. Details about the number of patients, design of the trial, statistical considerations, comparator drugs and so on should be kept firmly in the background. Highlight what the product can do for the doctor and the patient. Always remember: 'Sell the product, not the trial'.

Beware of questions about the 'Class Effect'

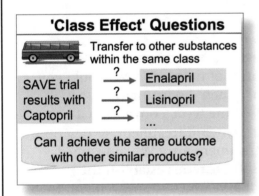

The 'class effect' refers to the potential interchangeability of substances within the same chemical class. Experts like to raise this sensitive issue during symposia and workshops: 'Can the study results be transferred to other substances within the same class?' or 'Can I achieve the same outcome with other similar products?'

One example involved a discussion about the clinical equivalence of ACE inhibitors (a class of antihypertensive drugs). The SAVE (Survival and Ventricular Enlargement) trial done with the ACE inhibitor Captopril showed results in favour of that substance. Captopril reduced the risk of mortality attributed to cardiovascular events by 21 percent.

Keep tight-lipped about theories

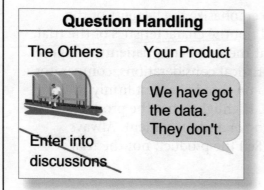

The company sponsoring the SAVE trial and subsequently marketing Captopril was Bristol-Myers-Squibb. When a representative was asked the 'class effect' question, his answer was along the following lines: 'We have the data, they don't' (with 'they' implying the competitors). Use similar statements if you are asked similar questions and leave it at that. This is one of the rare occasions when you should be absolutely tight-lipped. Resist the temptation to speculate. You have the scientific evidence and the other companies do not.

Learn the power of language

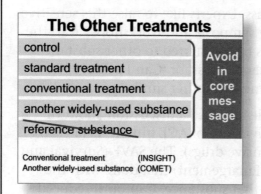

In your discussions, you may need to talk about alternative forms of therapy. How should you refer to them? When discussing the INSIGHT trial, Bayer used the term 'conventional treatment' or 'standard treatment' to describe the diuretic treatment arm. When justified by the results, these terms establish the expectation of a treatment improvement. In the COMET, Carvedilol or Metoprolol European Trial, metoprolol was referred to as 'another widely used substance', essentially a neutral description. You should avoid the term 'reference substance' because this implies the definitive treatment. Your final message should always highlight your product and not the other form of treatment.

Think positive

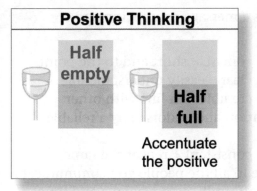

Successful marketers have a mindset that focuses on the positive. This is a useful approach for marketing clinical trials. Marketers don't consider the glass half empty; for them it is half full. They don't ignore negative aspects, but they are able to highlight the positive and desirable ones. Keeping the right balance between the two and appropriately representing the risk-benefit-ratio of a drug is an art that can be learned.

Capture the spirit

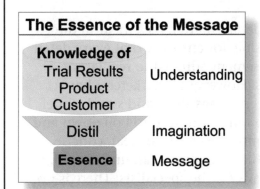

You need to distil your detailed knowledge:

- of the trial results
- of the product characteristics, and
- of the customers' needs

into its essence. This task requires understanding and imagination. A clear and original message is crucial if you are going to communicate your competitive advantage successfully to your customers.

Create a convincing message

A Convincing Message

Concise	Short and to the point
Clear	Easily understandable
Credible	Endorsed by reliable sources
Consistent	Repeated in a uniform way

What makes a message convincing and compelling?

- Make it concise = short and to the point
- Make it clear = easily understandable
- Make it credible = in line with other information and endorsed by a reliable source
- Make it consistent = repeat the same message to all the people you communicate with (uniformity across people and time).

Keep it simple

A Clear Message

	Keep things brief and clear
Everything is important	**Keep it short and simple**

I know that details matter. As a medical director, I was responsible for ensuring that every detail of an advertisement adhered to regulatory requirements. However as marketer, I have learned to keep things short and simple: brief is better than long. You need to boil down and condense complex issues into clear, concise and crisp claims that everybody can understand. Keep the details for the specialists. There is no need to say everything. If in doubt, compress, reduce, shorten, abridge and summarize.

Major Results of XYZ Trial

The clinical study of A versus B resulted in risk reductions of

Primary endpoint
- 8% in all-cause mortality (non-significant trend: p=0.128)

Secondary endpoints
- 12% in combined all-cause mortality and all-cause hospitalization (p=0.002)
- 10% in cardiovascular mortality (non-significant trend: p=0.073)
- 8% in combined all-cause mortality and cardiovascular hospitalization (p=0.036)
- 9% in combined cardiovascular mortality and hospitalization (p=0.027)
- 8% in fatal and non-fatal ... and hospitalization ... (p=0.374)

Post-hoc analysis
- 15% in combined all-cause mortality and hospitalisation ... (p<0.001)

This piece is based on a real example. The original trial name has been changed to 'XYZ Trial'. The readers cannot see the message when confronted with all this complex information, nor will they bother.

Check for clarity

A Clear Draft
Ask: Is your draft Easy to read? Easy to understand? Easy to remember?

Once you have developed a draft, please check:

- is it easy to read?
- is it easy to understand?
- is it easy to remember?

If you do not get a green light on all three items, change and simplify your draft.

Avoid pitfalls when developing content

The Main Pitfall
Saying more than is necessary and trying to put all the information into one single document

The most common mistake is to put too much information into one piece or document — whether it is an advertisement in a journal, a detail-aid folder for the sales force or a brochure for physicians. It is tempting for someone with a strong orientation toward research to try and cram too much information into a single document. These overloaded documents drown your message and your prospect will not even bother to read them.

Be concise

A Straightforward Message

Delete unnecessary items

Drop details that do not
convey your message

Eliminate words that do not sell

Principle in Direct Response Marketing

Keep everything you do straightforward. Avoid superfluous words, styles, symbols and images. Pull out all the stops in your language while making sure that you represent the right risk–benefit ratio of your drug. Do not communicate more than is necessary: too many cooks spoil the broth and too many details confuse your message. Eliminate any details that do not help you convey your message:

- use simple language
- cut any words that do not sell
- satisfy the need for a quick read.

Move from Features to Benefits

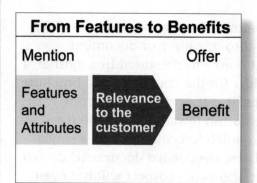

The customers are not interested in those features of your product or trial that have no relevance to their life (for example, details of statistical analysis). They are only interested in the potential benefits that you and your company can provide. Leaving human appreciation and financial rewards aside, your main benefit consists in solving a health problem.

Solve customers' problems

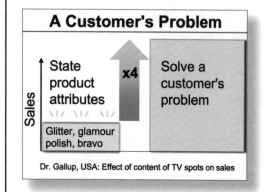

Dr Gallup investigated the effect of the content of televised commercials in the US on subsequent sales for certain consumer goods. He found that – compared to stating product attributes ('the glitter and the glamour') – commercials that purported to solve a customer's problem resulted in sales that were four times higher. The conclusion: solve a problem and increase revenue.

Offer solutions

Providing Solutions?

Nice products and nice trial results ...

... will not necessarily solve problems

Why should your customers care? Are you helping them solve a problem? Are you helping them to find an answer to a question in their professional lives? Do you meet an unmet need? Is there a fit between what your customer needs and what you offer?

A new pharmacological breakthrough or the amount of substance used per tablet do not qualify as elements of a solution. Case in point: one pharmaceutical company built their message around the small dosage the patients had needed to take. They had prominently displayed the term 'microdose' in their advertisement campaigns for a cardiovascular drug. They realized later that this feature does not lend itself to a convincing argument for the prescribing physician. They ultimately changed the slogan.

Follow the solution imperative

The Big Question

Product and trial results

Which problem do they solve?

Your offer must match the need

The following questions sound straightforward, but are essential to your success:

- which specific problems do you solve with your product and your trial results?
- are you sure that it is a problem or an unmet need for the doctor?

If your customers are not aware of a problem, they will not listen to you.

Work on these questions, until you have found a satisfactory answer.

You may need to sharpen doctors' awareness for particular problems. For example, companies marketing lipid-lowering drugs (especially statins) have successfully increased physicians' awareness of the risks of hyperlipidemia and the healthcare benefits of treating this condition resulting in tremendous product revenues.

Understand the real needs

The Doctor's Real Needs

My goals	The doctor is interested
	Improving patients' health
	Making patients happy
Giving state-of-the-art treatment	
Saving precious time	
Being financially successful	

Focus on the key areas in which doctors seek better solutions. Ensure that you provide the doctors you are targeting with solutions to the problems that concern them. Give them only the support they are really interested in.

Pin down your solution

The Dimensions of Your Offer

Your product	Improvements in
	Efficacy
	Tolerability
	Convenience
	Affordability

Where do you provide a solution?

For most diseases, there are four areas in which your product can provide a solution. It may offer improved:

- efficacy (desired pharmacological effect)
- tolerability (the profile of side effects)
- convenience (user-friendliness)
- affordability (price).

You need to identify which of these elements is true of your drug.

Communicate explicit benefits

An Explicit Benefit I

The new intra-venous formulation of Examplex requires a shorter duration of infusion → Examplex saves time

The illustration shows how a shorter duration of infusion for a new drug results in a clear advantage for the patient and the healthcare professional. He or she saves precious time. This may seem obvious to you, but spell it out. Do not leave it to the physician to work out how features translate into benefits. Specify the benefit clearly.

An Explicit Benefit II

Examplex has a longer duration of action for treating this dysfunction → More time for the right moment

See also **Marketing campaign for Cialis®**
Treatment of erectile dysfunction. Cialis® is trademark from Lilly

This example shows how the pharmacokinetic feature of a longer duration of action and a longer half-life translate into a clear benefit. The concept 'more time for the right moment' is successfully used by the company Lilly for their product Cialis® in the treatment of erectile dysfunction.

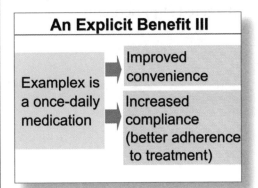

An Explicit Benefit III

Examplex is a once-daily medication → Improved convenience
→ Increased compliance (better adherence to treatment)

The once-daily administration of a medication results in better convenience and adherence to treatment (patient compliance) compared to a twice-daily medication.

Practical examples – The COMET Case Study

COMET: Scientific Data
Carvedilol in Heart Failure

In the Carvedilol or Metoprolol European Trial (COMET), around 3000 people with chronic heart failure were assigned to receive twice-daily doses of carvedilol or metoprolol for around five years. Yearly mortality rates were 8.3% with carvedilol and 10.0% with metoprolol. Average life-expectancy was eight years for patients given carvedilol compared with 6.6 years for patients assigned metoprolol. 34% of patients assigned carvedilol died during the five-year study compared with 40% of patients assigned metoprolol.

Based on presentations and The Lancet, 5 July 2003

The **C**arvedilol **or M**etoprolol **E**uropean **T**rial (COMET) included around 3000 people with chronic heart failure.

COMET: Message to Experts
Carvedilol in Heart Failure

Results of a European study in this week's issue of *The Lancet* suggest that the beta-blocker carvedilol offers substantial survival benefit compared with another widely-used beta blocker for the treatment of chronic heart failure.

Based on presentations and The Lancet, 5 July 2003

Based on these results, the company conveys a clear message targeted at experts and opinion leaders.

COMET: Message to Physicians
Carvedilol in Heart Failure

Dilatrend® patients live longer, on the average 1.4 years*

* COMET: Carvedilol *versus* Metoprololtartrat. The Lancet 2003;362:7-13

Dilatrend® is a trademark from Roche
Based on translation from German "Deutsches Ärzteblatt", 12 September 2003

A clear message targeted at prescribing physicians.

The ACTION Case Study

ACTION: Scientific Data

Long-Acting Nifedipine in Angina

A Coronary Disease **T**rial **I**nvestigating **O**utcome with **N**ifedipine GITS (ACTION): Patients with treated stable symptomatic coronary disease: 3825 patients assigned to nifedipine and 3840 assigned to placebo

Findings: 310 patients allocated nifedipine died compared with 291 people allocated placebo (p=0.41). Primary endpoint rates per 100 patient-years were 4.6 for nifedipine versus 4.75 for placebo. With nifedipine, rate of death and any cardiovascular event or procedure was 9.32 per 100 patient-years versus 10.50 for placebo (p=0.0012)

Based on presentations and The Lancet published online August 31, 2004

A Coronary Disease **T**rial **I**nvestigating **O**utcome with **N**ifedipine GITS (ACTION) investigated the effect of long-acting nifedipine in patients with coronary artery disease.

ACTION: Message to Experts

Long-Acting Nifedipine in Angina

Addition of nifedipine GITS to conventional treatment of angina pectoris has no effect on major cardiovascular event-free survival. Nifedipine GITS reduces the need for coronary angiography and interventions.

Based on presentations and The Lancet published online August 31, 2004

Based on these results, the company conveys a clear message targeted at experts and opinion leaders.

ACTION: Message to Physicians

Long-Acting Nifedipine in Angina

A unique study due to its design, size and scientific validity

Proven safety and improved outcomes on top of best practice treatment: 11% additional risk reduction*

*Primary endpoint and interventions

Based on presentations and The Lancet published online August 31, 2004

A clear message targeted at prescribing physicians

The 4'S' Case Study

4 'S': Scientific Data

Scandinavian Simvastatin Survival Study

Although noncardiac death rates were similar among the groups, the relative risk of mortality (from any cause) was decreased 30%, and the relative risk of coronary mortality was decreased 42% in the simvastatin arm.

Based on presentations and the article by Pedersen TR: Coronary artery disease: the Scandinavian Simvastatin Survival Study experience. Am J Cardiol. 1998 Nov 26;82(10B):53T-56T

4 'S': Message to Physicians

Scandinavian Simvastatin Survival Study

Zocor® Power for survival

Zocor® is a trademark from Merck & Co

The **S**candinavian **S**imvastatin **S**urvival **S**tudy investigated the effect of simvastatin in patients with hyperlipidemia.

Based on these results, the company conveys a clear message targeted at prescribing physicians.

The Examplex case study

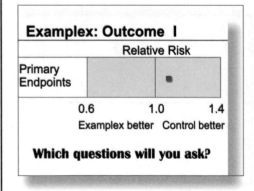

Our example company spent millions on a large international high-quality trial involving several thousand patients with a cardiovascular disease. We will call it the Examplex trial. The data were analysed.

You are the product manager responsible for product 'Examplex'. What set of questions will you ask? Subsequent illustrations show you how to use these questions to move through various drafts and arrive at a final version that provides a far more balanced view of the study results.

The Examplex case study (cont)

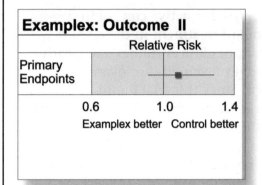

The answer to a question for your statistician or medical advisor: 'What are the statistical confidence intervals for these endpoints?' will result in this diagram.

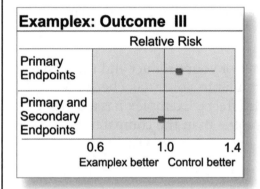

Asking your statistician or medical advisor 'What are the results for primary and secondary endpoints in this study?' results in this variation to the diagram.

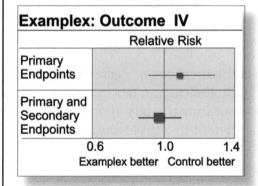

Asking your statistician or medical advisor 'How many of the individual data sets contribute to the primary and to the secondary endpoint?' results in this diagram. The diagram has now shifted in favour of your product, although you cannot construe a clinically relevant difference between the two treatment arms. Is this a fair representation? Yes it is, because the combined number of primary and secondary endpoints is usually more relevant to practising physicians who see the patients in their medical practice – independently of whether an endpoint met the required strict adherence to study protocol criteria which would qualify it as primary.

The Examplex case study (cont)

Examplex: Message

Examplex is effective in preventing cardiovascular complications:
An appropriate and safe initial treatment

The substance used as active control in this trial was standard treatment in the disease investigated. Prior clinical studies had clearly demonstrated it prevented cardiovascular complications. Since this trial found no relevant difference in efficacy between the active control and the substance Examplex, Examplex can be considered as having similar beneficial effects to the active control. This leads to the message expressed in the example.

Be sure to discuss this with your medical department and check regulatory requirements in your country before promoting any message.

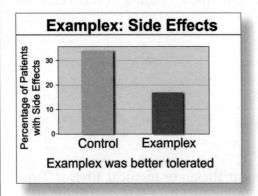

If the efficacies of your product and the active control are similar in your trial, check the profile of side effects. Examplex has a better tolerability profile than the comparator.

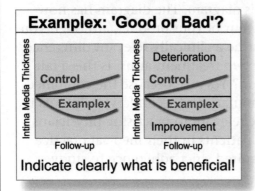

In some charts the increases or decreases of sonographic, radiological and laboratory parameters are not immediately apparent to the reader as a benefit or a disadvantage. You need to indicate clearly what is beneficial! The illustration shows one way to illustrate that the decrease in 'intima media thickness' associated with Examplex is indeed a desirable outcome. Place the word 'improvement' on the appropriate side of the horizontal axis so that the reader instantly recognizes this change as a favourable result.

Sell the product not the study

Brand Name Visibility
Brand name in study name?
Eventually 'rename' the study = Modify the study name
'Sell the product, not the study'

Is your product mentioned in the name of the trial? What do you do if your brand name is not part of the study name? You could 'rename' the study internally so it reflects your brand name. In most cases, it is enough simply to put the product name before the study name (usually an acronym) when you refer to it. For example, the name of your product is 'Examplex' and the acronym of the study is 'ABC'. Your clinical trial name becomes the 'Examplex ABC study'. Make sure your team agrees to use the new term consistently in all your internal and external material to ensure the biggest impact on prescribing behaviour.

A trial where the impact on sales of the substance investigated was very limited, was the HOT (Hypertension Optimal Treatment) trial – well known in the cardiovascular sector. However, only few prescribing physicians knew which was the main drug used in the trial (it was the calcium antagonist felodipine).

Know and respect statutory limits

Statutory Restrictions
Act responsibly and ethically:
Do **not** hide negative data!
Do **not** cover up negative results!
Publish **all** results whether positive or negative!

You should ensure compliance with all relevant standards. See chapter entitled 'Codes of Practice'. Your reputation and your credibility are your most valuable assets amongst your direct customers, the public and governmental agencies. Various incidents in late 2004 and early 2005 prompted government agencies to enact regulations that will require pharmaceutical companies to publish the trial results of all completed clinical trials that they have initiated. Companies that conceal trial results (for example, because they do not favour their product) are providing a disservice to their customers and their product.

Handle 'negative data' appropriately

Handling 'Negative' Data

The company Eli Lilly will publish **all** of its clinical trial results on its clinical trial registry
www.lillytrials.com

• Trial Results by Therapeutic Area
• Trial Results by Product
• Initiated Trials
• Recruiting Trials

One example for handling data from clinical trials is illustrated on the website www.lillytrials.com, where the company Eli Lilly will publish all of its clinical trial results. Visit this website to see how they do it.

Choose your words with care

Careless Wording

ABC & Co   Training Document
Potential Questions about Product Safety

Dodge
....
....

"... implying that sales reps were being taught to evade doctor's questions."

Based on a November 2004 article in The Wall Street Journal

Dictionary: to dodge = to keep away, to avoid

An article published in *The Wall Street Journal* commented on the use of the word 'dodge' in a company's training document that instructed sales representatives on how to deal with potential questions about the safety of their product. The training document could be interpreted as '... implying that sales representatives were being taught to evade doctors' questions.' The importance of responsible behaviour is obvious. In addition, be careful in your choice of words when writing your training manuals. Therefore watch what you write!

Beware careless emails

Careless Email

The Attorney ... filed civil fraud charges against the company, citing an e-mail written by company officials discussing ...

... the need to effectively manage the dissemination of data in order to minimize any potential negative commercial impact.

The Washington Post carried an article (26 August 2004) describing how the New York Attorney General Eliot L. Spitzer filed civil fraud charges against a big pharmaceutical company while citing an email in which company officials discussed certain studies and the need to manage effectively the dissemination of data in order to minimize any potential negative commercial impact. This incident shows how careless behaviour and careless emails can be loose cannonballs which can lead to legal proceedings against you and your company.

WINNING ATTENTION

Give impact

Lack of Impact

Major reason: Recipients ...

?	
... did not believe your claims	... did not see or did not notice or did not bother to read your stuff

What is the most valuable resource of all?

It is our time and attention, because they are very limited and once spent, we can never get them back. The most common reason why direct mail generates poor response rates is simply that the recipients didn't see, didn't notice or didn't bother to read your message. Winning your prospects' attention is where you need to start. If you don't initially capture their attention, you will fail – no matter how brilliant your piece may be.

Capture attention

Attention Grabbing

Curious	It does not matter what your message is ..
	if you cannot capture the prospect's attention in the first place
	Make viewer interested

The first step in influencing prescribing behaviour is gaining your prospect's attention. No one was ever excited by a book they weren't moved to open! You need to ensure that the prospect notices your activities. Everything else is futile if you do not capture their attention.

Get the reader's interest.

Apply proven eye-catchers in your documents

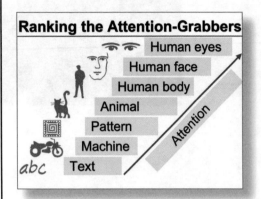

There are certain visual elements you can use in your printed material to grab the attention of the observer or reader. Some advertising agencies ignore this fact and use non-relevant objects in their campaigns which means they miss an excellent opportunity to win attention. Pictures of the human face and the human eyes are the top two attention-winning items. If you analyse outdoor advertising (for example, posters) for fast-moving consumer goods, you will frequently find these two elements in prominent positions. Make sure the images you use are relevant, campaignable and attention-grabbing.

Emphasize uniqueness

Who was the first man to walk on the moon? I have asked this questions many times in my seminars and the right answer invariably comes up: the astronaut Neil Armstrong (in 1969). But then I ask the participants: who was the second man on the moon? Very few of them remember Buzz Aldrin. We usually remember who was the first person who achieved something. Remembering those who followed in their footsteps is much less likely.

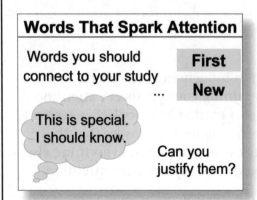

There are two words that spark attention and imply that your study is special: 'New' and 'First'. Use them and you increase the probability that your text will be read. If you can connect these words to your study appropriately, they will make the listener or reader want to know more about it. The word 'first' is preferable. If you were the first to do a particular study, it does not matter how many similar studies follow. The word 'new' needs to be time limited to a short period following the release of the study results. In some European countries, you are allowed by law to use 'new' only if your results are less than 12 months old. Make sure your use of 'new' and 'first' is correct and justified.

Emphasize uniqueness (cont)

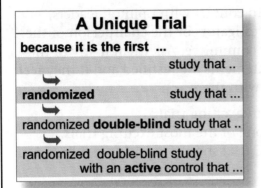

A Unique Trial

because it is the first ...

                  study that ..

➥

randomized   study that ...

➥

randomized **double-blind** study that ..

➥

randomized double-blind study
           with an **active** control that ...

'My study is similar to many previous studies, which means it is neither first nor unique' – I have often heard this sentence. Although not obvious at first glance, many studies are special or distinct in some regard. There are some questions that can help you identify the unique aspect and justify a claim of 'first'. Look carefully at the design, numbers of patients and other characteristics of your trial. It may not be the first one to address a particular question, but it may be the first randomized study, since the other ones were case control studies. Or it may be the first randomized double-blind study, since the other ones were open-label. Or it may be the first randomized double-blind study using an active control, since the other ones were placebo-controlled.

The First Study Investigating

Treatment of hypertension ...

➥

Fixed combination hypertension treatment ...

➥

Fixed **low-dose** combination hypertension treatment ...

➥

Initial fixed low-dose combination hypertension treatment ...

This example shows a different set of features that help you to find a unique selling proposition for your trial, which then allows you to attach the important word 'first' to your study.

The Largest Study

The largest morbidity and mortality study in long-term use of ACE inhibitors in the secondary prevention of stable angina

EUROPA
European Trial on reduction of cardiac events with perindopril in stable coronary artery disease

Translated from a German advertisement
Coversum® is a trademark from Servier

Your study may not be the first, but it may be the largest study investigating a particular question.

Add attractive adjectives when appropriate

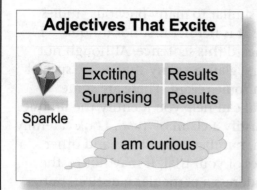

You may be in contact with opinion leaders, principal investigators or the chairperson of the trial steering committee. Ask them if any of the following statements are justified and if they feel comfortable with them.

- 'ABC is an exciting trial.'
- 'ABC is one of the most exciting trials.'
- 'The ABC trial shows surprising results.'
- 'The ABC trial is a fascinating study.'

Note: All of these statements are based on real quotations. Using them helps you to ensure that the study gets the attention it deserves. As before, make sure they are justified by asking the appropriate questions.

Use precise numbers

Precise Numbers	
Key conclusions from the Examplex trial in diabetic patients	The **3** key conclusions from the Examplex trial in diabetic patients

Many books, especially in the self-help and personal growth sector, use precise numbers in their titles to arouse the prospect's curiosity. For example, 'The 22 Immutable Laws of Branding' or 'Seven Habits of Highly Successful People'.

The example shows how you could change the initial draft title of a brochure to win more attention and arouse more curiosity. The reader finds three key conclusions intriguing and is motivated to find out more, and read whatever follows.

Be culturally sensitive

You need to avoid certain numbers in certain countries or regions. The number four spells bad luck in China and the number '13' spells bad luck in many Western countries. Research in direct marketing has shown, that an uneven number usually elicits higher response rates than an even number.

Offer practical tips to the reader

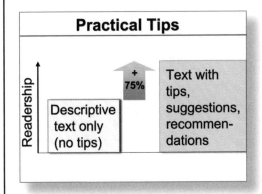

Giving practical tips, suggestions or recommendations can increase the readership of your text by as much as 75 per cent. Add a section to your text that does just that. When marketing a product against high blood pressure, you could insert a short section in your detail aid folders. This section reminds doctors to offer advice to their patients to develop a healthier lifestyle, for example:

- stop smoking
- maintain regular physical exercise
- eat a balanced diet
- ease stress.

MAKING BEST USE OF LANGUAGE

Develop the complete package to convey your message

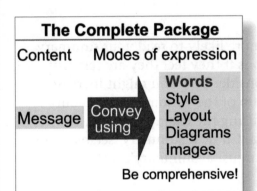

The Complete Package

Content   Modes of expression

Message   Convey using → **Words** Style Layout Diagrams Images

Be comprehensive!

You have various ways to express the content of your communication. Use the complete spectrum to convey your message effectively. Choose the appropriate words, style, layout, diagrams and images and the right combination of these components.

Find the right vocabulary

Verbal Gems

Find the verbal gems

Words that convey your message effectively are precious.

Words can be very powerful. Look for the words that best convey your message. Sounds easy – but remember, there are people working in communication agencies that make a living out of finding those verbal gems and developing the right vocabulary.

Be clear and convincing

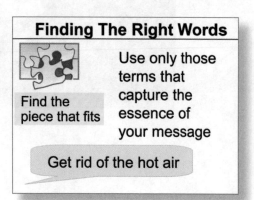

Find the words that fit. Identify those terms that capture the essence of your message. Use vocabulary that is to the point. Be selective in your choice of words and get rid of the words that do not help to convey your message.

Tailor your headlines

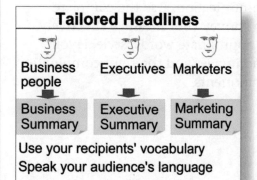

People are more likely to read your summary or conclusions if they feel they are relevant to them. Consider how you might increase the readership of the various parts of your documents using the examples given. For physicians, a 'Clinical Summary' seems more relevant than just a 'Summary'.

Evoke an emotional response

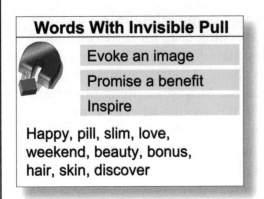

Words With Invisible Pull

Evoke an image

Promise a benefit

Inspire

Happy, pill, slim, love, weekend, beauty, bonus, hair, skin, discover

There are words that have a subtle, invisible pull – similar to the attraction a magnet exerts on iron. These are words that evoke the imagination, promise a benefit, inspire, reassure or trigger certain emotional reactions.

Evoke imagination if the evidence supports it

Words Easy to Imagine	
Slimming Pill	Xenical®
Love Pill	Viagra®
Weekend Pill	Cialis®
Pill with Beauty Bonus	Valette®

Xenical® from Roche, Viagra® from Pfizer, Cialis® from Lilly, Valette® from Jenapharm

Look for words that create a mental picture and that help convey your message persuasively. You may sharpen awareness for the disease and its treatment but it would be unethical to attempt to create unnecessary demand. Be sure to adhere to the Codes of Practice.

Journalists frequently use terms in the media, where two well-known drugs for erectile dysfunction are often referred to as 'the love pill' and 'the weekend pill'.

Capture the imagination

Terms Easy to Imagine	
Anti-androgenic effect	Beneficial influence on hair and skin
	Ad for hormonal contraceptive
Proton Pump Inhibitor	Acid Pump Inhibitor
	Losec® of AstraZeneca

The term 'proton pump inhibitor' used to describe a top-selling drug for the treatment of gastrointestinal ulcers whilst scientifically accurate was changed to 'acid pump inhibitor' for a good reason. Most prescribing physicians are unlikely to have a clue what a 'proton pump' is. On the other hand, they can well imagine that an 'acid pump' is a pump producing acid in the gastrointestinal tract.

Learn the 'magic' words

The 'Magic' Words		
Imply a benefit	Benefit	Know-how
	Value	Success
	Advantage	Result
	Free	to win
	Health	to lead
I feel comfortable with ...		

There are buzz words or expressions that promise a benefit and that have been shown to increase response in direct mail campaigns. Pick the ones you feel comfortable with and use them in your promotional activities. This takes time and effort. Use these words only if the scientific evidence supports their use.

Establish a trial vocabulary

Vocabulary for Professionals

The ten most important words
for marketing the trial are ...

- •   •
- •   •
- •   •
- •   •

Write your 'trial dictionary'

One of the most valuable global brands is Coca-Cola. The company headquarters in Atlanta, Georgia, USA, has issued clear directives about the words to use in all promotional activities, the 'brand vocabulary'. Developing a consistent brand vocabulary reduces the risk of people employing a confusing and diffuse range of words or expressions to convey the brand message.

The exact set of words you use in the promotional material for pharmaceutical products is, of course, limited by national or international regulations. Narrow the key words down to a list of approximately 10 to 15. Using this common vocabulary will ensure a consistent terminology in all your promotional activities including the messages conveyed by your sales force and your public relations department.

Check your brand vocabulary

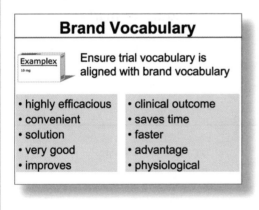

Brand Vocabulary

Examplex
10 mg

Ensure trial vocabulary is aligned with brand vocabulary

- • highly efficacious
- • convenient
- • solution
- • very good
- • improves

- • clinical outcome
- • saves time
- • faster
- • advantage
- • physiological

You need to ensure that your trial vocabulary and your brand vocabulary share common words. A common vocabulary will increase the consistency and therefore the impact of your communication.

Have you checked the alignment of your trial and brand vocabulary?

Build a vocabulary for the press

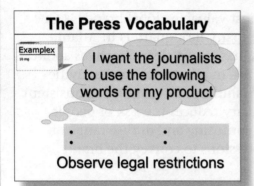

The Press Vocabulary

Examplex
10 mg

I want the journalists to use the following words for my product

:   :

Observe legal restrictions

Which words and phrases do you want the journalists to use when they cover your product in the media? Remember to check with your regulatory department which wording you may use. Be sure to adhere to the Codes of Practice.

Avoid loaded words

Loaded Words

Drop *barbed wire* words with negative implications

Avoid hazardous language

- Problematic
- Difficult
- Complicated
- Questionable
- Mistake

People are particularly turned off by words with negative implications such as 'problematic' and 'difficult', because they have enough problems and difficulties of their own. 'Mistake' often implies that somebody is to blame which is seldom helpful. And never use condescending terms for your study, product, or market.

Beware of arrogance

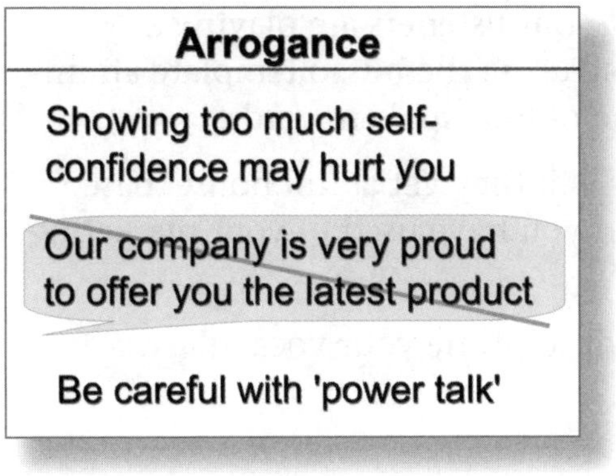

Arrogance

Showing too much self-confidence may hurt you

Our company is very proud to offer you the latest product

Be careful with 'power talk'

Statements that exude too much confidence or pride can be damaging. Your prospects do not expect you to undersell yourselves, but statements that could be interpreted as vain, self-important, or arrogant will certainly turn them off.

Avoid clichés

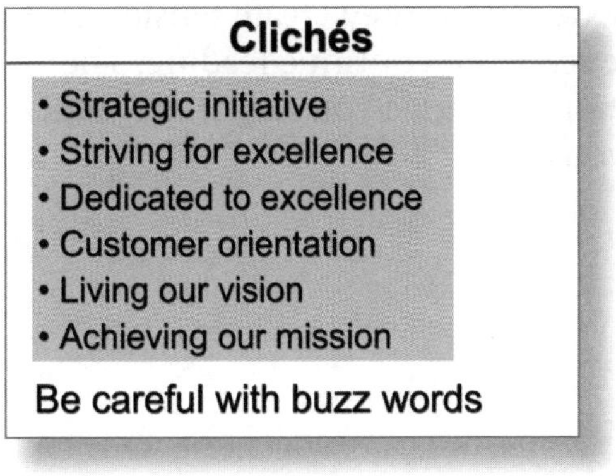

Clichés

- Strategic initiative
- Striving for excellence
- Dedicated to excellence
- Customer orientation
- Living our vision
- Achieving our mission

Be careful with buzz words

Certain catchy phrases or terms have been over-used and become clichéd. The trouble with corporate jargon is that people don't believe or understand it.

Use buzz words selectively and with care; avoid clichés and jargon.

Beware of jargon

'Corporatese': The Game

Bull Shit Bingo: Fictional game to be played during boring corporate meetings filled with buzzwords to stop people falling asleep.

Synergy	Proactive	Assets	Benchmark
Strategic Fit	Win-Win	Dynamic	Value-Added
Gap Analysis	Fast Track	Critical Path	Total Quality
Best Practice	Empower	Leverage	Client Focus

Aim: Form a line of four spoken words

Imagine that your listeners are playing a fictional game using the bingo template aiming to form a line of four spoken words.

How quickly will they get a 'full house' based on the jargon you have used in your marketing activities?

You may want to prune your vocabulary.

Plan an inner logic in your texts

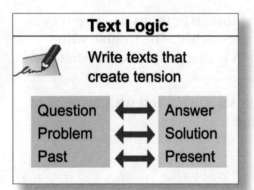

Text Logic

Write texts that create tension

Question	Answer
Problem	Solution
Past	Present

Write your texts so that they create tension and stimulate the reader to continue reading. The next illustrations will give you examples. Which method do you prefer?

Questions and Answers

Wouldn't it be nice if you could forget your problem for 24 hours?

Examplex treats your problem for the next 24 hours

Based on a real advertisement
Remember the legal constraints

Ask a question and then give the answer. Devise your questions in a way that allows you to offer the answers you want the readers to take away with them.

Plan an inner logic in your texts (cont)

Problems and Solutions

Hypertension-induced cardiovascular morbidity is a healthcare concern.

Examplex can effectively control hypertension and help to reduce cardiovascular morbidity.

Describe a problem and then explain why your study or product provides a solution.

Past and Present 1

Many cancer patients suffer | Problem
from bone-destroying activities associated with bone metastases.

Until recently, there was no | Solution
effective treatment for bone metastases. **Now** biphosphonates can help improve bone strength in cancer patients.

The 'Past and Present' is a similar technique to the 'Problems and Solutions'. In this case, you emphasize the dimension of time and describe how therapy has developed from a gloomy past to a bright present, highlighting your product appropriately.

Past and Present 2

Diabetes is with your | Problem
patients all day, every day.

Now there's an insulin | Solution
that can work just as long. Examplex provides 24-hour coverage with just one administration.

Based on a real advertisement

A dramatic problem needs a convincing solution: Examplex.

Remember Zarathustra

The advice given by Zarathustra about 3000 years ago is still relevant today. It applies both to spoken and to written communication:

- speak the truth, but speak it pleasantly.
- do not speak an unpleasant truth.
- never utter a pleasant untruth.

Beware of hidden connotations

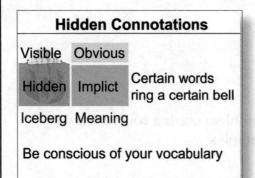

There are some words that have a hidden or implicit meaning, often sexual or negative. Sometimes this hidden meaning is detectable only when the word is spoken or slightly mispronounced. Make sure that you check with native speakers whenever you are delivering a message in a language other than your own.

Use positive language

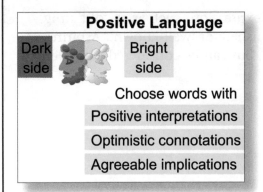

You can often describe a situation with negative or with positive words. Improve your vocabulary. Choose uplifting words with a positive meaning, an optimistic connotation and an agreeable implication. To your readers, 'do' is far more powerful than 'don't'.

Accentuate the positive and keep a fair balance

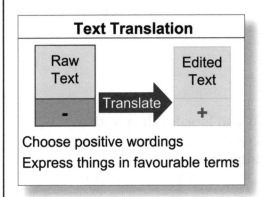

Make a conscious effort to replace negative words. This does not mean that all your words should be cheerful, rosy or sugar-coated. Check back with your medical department on a regular basis. Ask your medical colleagues for a copy of the draft version of the trial report or the manuscript of a planned article before they start the final approval process. They are unlikely to offer these documents without prompting. Therefore, please ask them. Don't be afraid to suggest subtle changes in grammar and vocabulary in the 'summary' or 'conclusions' sections. Shorten sentences so they are easier for journalists to quote. Check if you can insert words like 'value' or 'benefit' when appropriate. Check if you can replace any negative words with words that have more positive meaning.

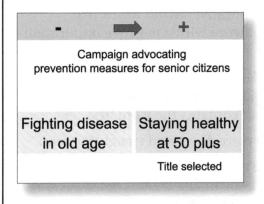

The US Government were looking for an optimistic title for their new campaign advocating health improvement amongst senior citizens. Instead of saying 'Fighting disease in old age' they chose the encouraging title 'Staying healthy at 50 plus'.

Accentuate the positive and keep a fair balance (cont)

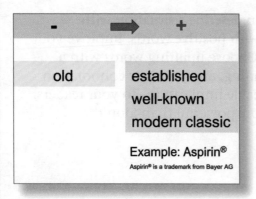

Avoid using expressions such as an 'old' drug. Call it 'established' or 'well-known'. Aspirin® may be 'old', but can be considered a 'modern classic'.

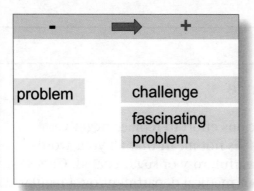

Replace negative words by positive ones. 'Problems' turn into 'challenges'. If you have a really big problem, how about a 'fascinating problem'?

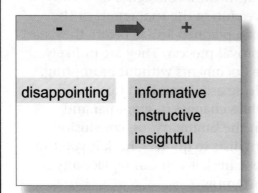

Edit your texts and look for the positive. People might call your trial results 'negative' or 'disappointing'. You should call them 'informative', 'instructive' or 'insightful'.

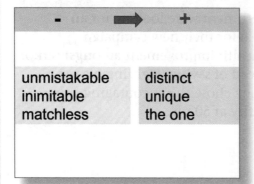

Eliminate the negative. Avoid words that contain a root word with a negative implication. For example:

- 'unmistakable' contains the word 'mistake'
- 'inimitable' contains the word 'imitate'
- 'matchless' contains the word 'less'.

Use words that are direct and straightforward:

- 'a unique trial'
- 'a distinct advantage'
- 'the one product that ...'.

Accentuate the positive and keep a fair balance (cont)

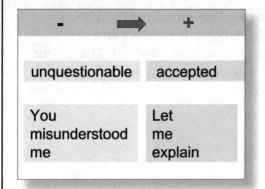

The sentence 'It is unquestionable that ...' contains the word 'question'. You can express it more directly by stating 'It is well accepted that ...'.

'You misunderstood me' implies a lack of understanding from the other person and may sound abrasive. The sentence 'Let me explain' sounds more polite and welcoming. The other person will then be more receptive to your statements.

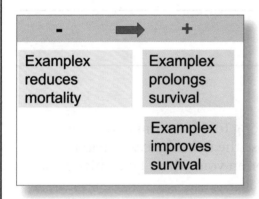

Survival sounds better than mortality. You may want to move from 'Examplex reduces mortality' to 'Examplex prolongs survival' or 'Examplex improves survival'.

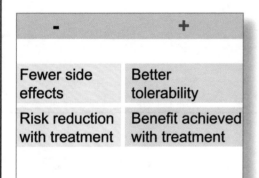

'Tolerability' sounds less threatening than 'side effects'. You may want to move from 'side effect profile' to 'tolerability profile'.

'Benefit' sounds more positive than 'risk reduction'. However it is also less specific. So in this instance you may wish to stick with the more specific term 'risk reduction'. An option is using 'benefit' in the title and creating a subtitle mentioning 'risk reduction'.

Be affirmative

Affirmative Statements

You deny	You affirm
not contaminated	pure
at no charge	free

Be direct and straightforward

Avoid statements that contain negatives or denials. Use affirmative, direct and straightforward statements instead. Thus, 'Our product is not contaminated' becomes 'Our product is pure'.

Always choose concision

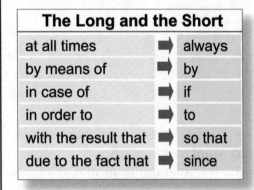

The Long and the Short

at all times	➡	always
by means of	➡	by
in case of	➡	if
in order to	➡	to
with the result that	➡	so that
due to the fact that	➡	since

Move from long to short terms and phrases. Always choose the more concise version. This will shorten your whole text which makes it faster to read.

Emphasize the benefits

Emphasizing Benefits	
What the company does	What the customer gets
We will send you a free book	You will receive a free book
We will mail you the patient brochures	You can offer brochures to your patients

It is clear that you must communicate the appropriate risk-benefit ratio of your product. The following chapters give suggestions on how to use words that will make your communication more effective.

Phrase your messages from the customer's standpoint, not from the company's point of view. The customer is not interested in what you do, but in how she or he will benefit. Thus, 'We will send you a book' becomes 'You will receive a free book' and 'We will mail you the patient brochures' becomes 'You can offer brochures to your patients'.

Find alternatives to 'prove'

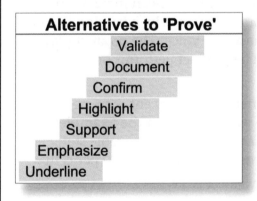

Alternatives to 'Prove'
Validate
Document
Confirm
Highlight
Support
Emphasize
Underline

The term 'prove' may be used correctly in the context of mathematics or of logic, but not in describing the conclusions of a clinical trial. There is always a certain probability of error. If this risk of error is estimated to be below 5 per cent, the conclusion is usually referred to as 'statistically significant'. Avoid potential legal problems and replace 'prove' with other terms.

Replace 'difference'

Alternatives to 'Difference'

Case: Examplex is 20% better

20% improvement

20% increase

20% difference

When you use the term 'difference', your listener or reader does not know the direction of the change. Even if you use 'increase' or 'decrease', you will need additional words in order to make it clear whether you are talking about a beneficial or a detrimental effect, a favourable or unfavourable outcome. You may therefore prefer the word 'improvement', if the context allows. The listener or reader will then know instantly that you are talking about a benefit.

Use the active voice

The Active Voice

A 20% increase in survival rate was observed in the Examplex group	Examplex improved survival by 20%

SAVE trial: Captopril improved ... by 20%

Grammar does matter. You can increase the impact of your statements by changing from the passive to the active voice. The product plays an active part. The product performs or achieves something.

So the statement 'A 20 per cent increase in survival rate was observed in the Examplex group' becomes the more memorable statement 'Examplex improved survival by 20 per cent'.

Edit your scientific texts

Text Editing
This randomized clinical trial investigated the influence of substantin on the mortality of patients with breast cancer. The trial showed a significant difference between the treatment arms in favour of substantin.
Substantin significantly improves survival in breast cancer patients. The results of this randomized clinical trial clearly confirm the benefit of substantin.

Sometimes you will need to edit and revise the original scientific texts in order to make the texts in your materials clearer and shorter. Discuss the suggested changes with the principal investigators, the authors of the publication and your medical colleagues. Get their agreement. If they say 'Basically this is the same as what I had written', you know that you have done a good job.

Convert 'blind' headlines

Avoid 'Blind' Headlines
Use headlines that: • Promise to add value • Mention an advantage • Announce a benefit
Let the sun shine in

Headlines are 'blind', when they fail to add value, to mention an advantage or to announce a benefit. Instead of using a 'blind' headline, let the light in.

Always use an appropriate interesting headline for your texts, one that

- promises to add value
- mentions an advantage
- announces a benefit.

Sir David Ogilvy, a guru amongst advertisers, was known to test as many as 16 different versions of headlines to find the most effective. Have a look at the headlines of your past folders, advertisements, or press releases. Can you improve on them in the future?

Insert pertinent subheadings

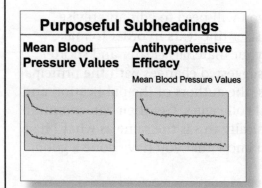

Purposeful Subheadings

Mean Blood Pressure Values	Antihypertensive Efficacy
	Mean Blood Pressure Values

How can you can change a descriptive title into one that promises a benefit? Using a new subtitle or subheading gives the pertinent information and guides the reader. Alternatively, you can also use subheadings to pique the reader's curiosity.

Post your vocabulary

Visible 'Brand Dictionary'

The ten most important words for marketing the trial are ...

Write your vocabulary

Put in on the wall or computer

Make your brand and trial vocabulary very visible. Tape your brand dictionary to your computer screen or write it in large letters on flip chart paper and attach it to the wall of your office. Think of ways to constantly remind yourself and other people of the 'right' words.

DESIGN: CHOOSING STYLE

Make use of bullets

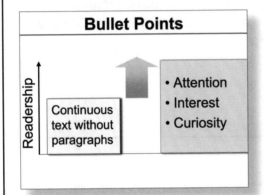

A continuous block of text will attract less readers than a well designed list. Use bullet points to express the key areas you wish to highlight. You will increase the likelihood that they are read.

Try lists of three

Lists of Three

- Liberté, fraternité, égalité
- Ready, set, go
- Many people cannot remember more than 3 items

Is there an optimal number of bullet points? Many people have trouble remembering more than three items, so use lists of three. If you want to list more than three items, uneven numbers of bullet points (for example five) will encourage higher response rates than even numbers.

Choose suitable symbols

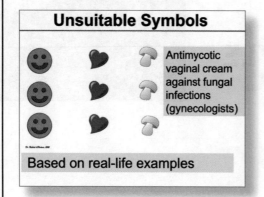

Cardiologists have a different view of the anatomy of the human heart than the stereotypical symbols some creative agencies love to use. The company that used mushrooms as symbols in their mailing promoting a vaginal cream designed to treat fungal infections, simply looked silly in the eyes of the targeted gynaecologists who received the mailing.

Using the typical well-established round symbols is the better technique. Squares and arrows are an option, but angular shapes usually appear less appealing than rounded shapes. You may have noticed that most pictograms and symbols in Microsoft Windows® XP have rounded shapes.

Use notes to annotate

Your Own Notes

Results of the randomized ABC trial in diabetic patients ...

Text that few people will ever read

Interesting Points
- •
- •
- •

Most people will not read the whole text of a scientific article. You can add your own notes highlighting important items. Bullet points will help the reader get the message. Select a heading other than those used in the original article: 'Conclusions', 'Summary, or 'Key points'. You could even print your text on adhesive Post-it® notes and stick them onto the original article. A Post-it® will catch the reader's attention.

Pay attention to typography

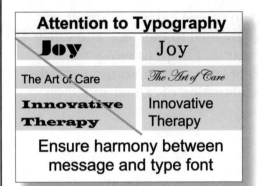

If you have precise branding guidelines, the decision about which fonts to use has already been made for you. Follow your branding guidelines. If the guidelines do not give any recommendations, alert your global brand team. If there is none, choose a font and stick to it.

Try to achieve a synergy between the message you want to convey and the font you use. Reaching consistency between content and typography is subjective. Do not decide on the font on your own and don't let your agency decide on their own. Have several versions available and ask some colleagues and clients.

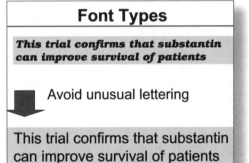

Avoid lettering that might appear unusual, eccentric, odd, outdated or strange.

Choose fonts that appear appropriate, modern and normal.

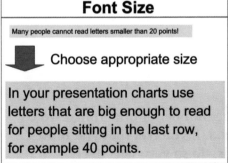

Choose an appropriate, easily readable font size. Many young creative people in advertising agencies have a tendency towards small font sizes. And yet many people over 40 (probably the vast majority of your customers) are far-sighted which means they will not be able to read small print without their reading glasses. Your printed text needs to be large enough so that they can read it even if they have misplaced their reading glasses. Presentation charts and print material demand of course specific guidelines.

Pay attention to typography (cont)

Capitals and Lower Case

THIS TRIAL CONFIRMS THAT SUBSTANTIN CAN IMPROVE SURVIVAL OF PATIENTS

 Avoid capital letters

This trial confirms that substantin can improve survival of patients

Text set solely in capital letters is difficult to read, since we are used to the 'peak and valley' silhouette of text that helps us recognize combinations of letters. Use an orthodox style, one with a combination of capital and lower case letters.

Bold Fonts

This trial **confirms** that **substantin** can **improve survival** of **patients**

 Restrict use of bold letters within the text

This trial confirms that substantin can **improve survival** of patients

Overuse of bold font makes the text difficult to read. Use bold type face sparingly and selectively. Reserve bold font for the words that convey a benefit to the reader.

Italics

This trial confirms that substantin can improve survival of patients with advanced breast cancer

 Stay away from italic style

This trial confirms that substantin can improve survival of patients with advanced breast cancer

Text set solely in italic is difficult to read and therefore best to avoid. If you feel that you must use it, do so very selectively.

Underlining

This <u>trial</u> <u>confirms</u> that <u>substantin</u> can <u>improve</u> <u>survival</u> of <u>patients</u> with advanced <u>breast cancer</u>

 Avoid underlining

This trial confirms that substantin can improve survival of patients with advanced breast cancer

Text with a large number of underlined words is difficult to read. If you feel that you must underline words, do so very selectively.

Opt for narrow columns

Column Width

This trial confirms that substantin can improve survival of patients with advanced breast cancer

 Limit the number of words within one line

This trial confirms that substantin can improve survival of patients with advanced breast cancer

Wide columns are difficult to read. Choose a narrow column width. Have a look at newspapers: they often have less than 30 characters per line. Visit professional websites. They, too, have narrow text columns. Of course you need to be careful to choose the appropriate column width. Too narrow can be as bad as too wide.

Choose reader-friendly line spacing

Line Spacing

This trial confirms that substantin can improve survival of patients with advanced breast cancer

 Set line spacing between 1.0 and 1.2

This trial confirms that substantin can improve survival of patients with advanced breast cancer

Generally do not set your line spacing below a value of 1.0. Choose line spacings between 1.0 and 1.2. Experiment and check which setting gives you best readability.

Contrast text and background

Text and Background

Dark-coloured letters on a dark-coloured background | Light-coloured letters on a light-coloured background

 Ensure sufficient contrast

Better readability | Better readability

Avoid dark-coloured letters on a dark-coloured background or light-coloured letters on a light-coloured background. Ensure sufficient contrast. Sounds obvious? How many folders, leaflets and advertisements violate this simple principle?

Use initial capitals

Initial Capitals	
Capitalize the first letter of the first word in a paragraph	Capitalize the first letter of the first word in a paragraph ...
	... and increase readership

Use an initial capital for the first letter of the paragraph: you will increase the likelihood that the viewer will start reading.

Use direct quotations

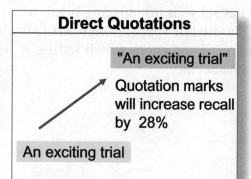

When you have a quotation or testimonial, use quotation marks. It makes the text more memorable. Encourage customers to contribute quotations and testimonials. Pick the most appropriate ones.

DESIGN: LAYOUT

The importance of layout

Layout is the geometrical arrangement of elements in a printed document. It is the composition of text and images and has been described as the architecture of the page. You can use it to your advantage.

Use the white space

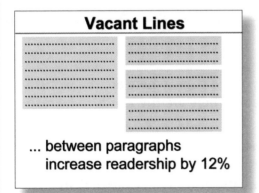

Vacant Lines

... between paragraphs increase readership by 12%

Vacant lines between your paragraphs help structure the text blocks. You increase readership by creating several short sections. Try to introduce a vacant line after every three to five lines of text. Think about the value of the white space on the page, as well as the text itself.

How to combine pictures and text

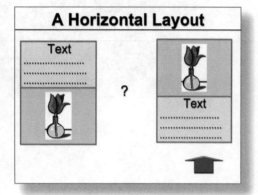

If you use an attention-grabbing element such as a picture in the bottom half of the page, it will draw the reader's eye towards that part of the page, too. The reader often will not return to the text. Normally text works more effectively if set below the picture.

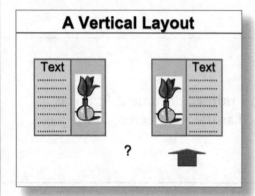

If you use an attention-grabbing element such as a picture in the right-hand side of the page, it will draw the reader's eye toward the right margin of the page. Remember the majority of languages are read from left to right, so put your picture on the left and the text on the right. The layout on double pages follows special rules, for example people should always look toward the centre.

Put key elements in key spots

Precious Space	
Which are the **first** and which are the **second** elements to be read in a piece?	
Headline	1
First words of copy	
Last words of copy	
Words underneath the photo	2

In the layout of the page, where are the words to be read first and where are the words to be read second?

Usually the reader starts with the headline, followed by the words underneath the picture. These spots are precious in any piece. Don't waste them with descriptions of little relevance. Use these two places to plant your key messages.

Use captions with care

Here are two examples: the one on the right is more effective than the one on the left. The message 'Examplex saves time' should be put below the picture, where it is most likely to be read. You will find the captions printed underneath images in newspapers. Pictures should always be accompanied by a caption! Make use of the space underneath the picture to place your most important message.

Avoid the pitfall of putting text above or inside the frame of a picture and avoid text that simply states the obvious. Make sure your main message is placed underneath and is directly relevant to the picture. If the text and picture don't match, find a more appropriate picture.

Stretch your headlines

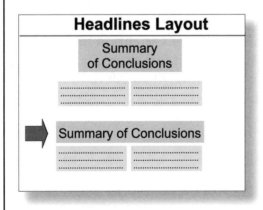

Research in direct-response marketing has shown the most effective way to achieve response with a 'guarantee' statement is to stretch it across the page. This form of layout exudes more confidence. If you apply this concept to the 'Conclusions', 'Key Points' or 'Executive Summary' sections of your document, you are better off making the layout of the headline wider than taller.

Work and rework your layout

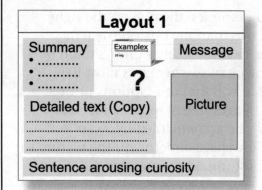

This example combines many of the pitfalls we discussed in the previous sections. The summary should be moved to the right. The picture and detailed text should be switched around. The message could be placed underneath the picture. The teaser sentence becomes the headline. The image of the package should be moved to the bottom right-hand corner.

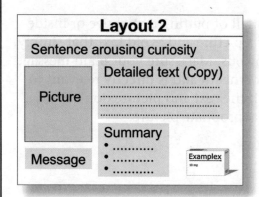

Here is an example of an improved layout. Bear in mind that there are many different ways of achieving impact with layout. Follow your branding guidelines. If you don't have them, develop several versions, test them and choose the format that works best for you. Then stick to it.

Make use of a Johnson Box

> ### A Johnson Box
>
> Aircraft designers tested various layouts. They found that
>
> drawing a box around a piece
>
> of text made it easier for pilots to find and to read the text.
>
> Graphic designers often use this technique in direct mail letters.

Drawing a frame around a piece of text will invariably draw the reader's attention to the framed text. As with most text design features, you need to use it sparingly to achieve the greatest effect.

DESIGNING DIAGRAMS AND CHARTS

Follow your reader's eyes

Recall with Substantin 1

Increase	Constant	Decrease
50%	48%	2%

Sequence of columns?

The order of columns in this table is ineffective. Your eyes move from the top left to the bottom right of a page and consequently the word 'Decrease' (the least important one) sticks in the reader's mind whilst the word 'Increase' (the more important) is lost.

Recall with Substantin 2

Decrease	Constant	Increase
2%	48%	50%

Appropriate way of depicting data?

Rearranging the columns results in a version of the table that draws more attention to 'Increase' and makes it more memorable. But, ask yourself, is a table the most appropriate way to illustrate the data?

Recall with Substantin 3

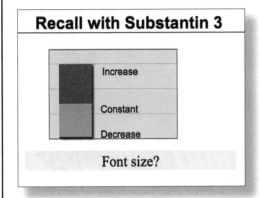

Font size?

This diagram conveys the message more effectively than a table. However, the sizes of the letters are out of proportion to the relevance of the group they describe.

Use your fonts to reinforce your message

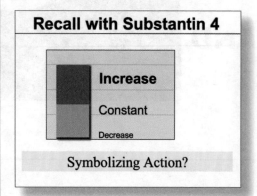

This diagram shows font sizes that are in proportion to the relevance of the group they describe. But, the diagram looks static. You might add a simple symbol to illustrate action and dynamics.

Introduce a dynamic

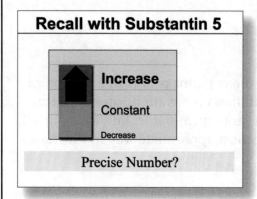

The upward arrow shows the direction of the change ('increase') and emphasizes the dynamic nature of the product. However, the precise degree of change remains unclear.

Be precise

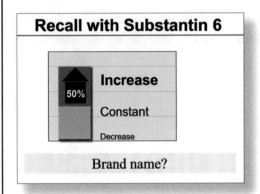

Ask yourself: What is the one number you want to convey? The one number the reader should remember is now in the arrow. Never display two numbers prominently.

One is enough. However, the reader's mind still remains unclear about the name of your product.

Use the brand name

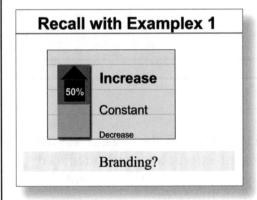

If the scientific context allows, swap the substance name (here 'Substantin') with the brand name (here 'Examplex'). Remember, your brand includes more than just a name. The brand name needs to be represented with an approved style, colour, font type and so on.

Strengthen your brand

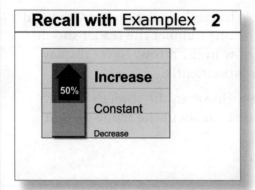

This diagram is one example of enhanced layout and design depicting the benefit of the brand.

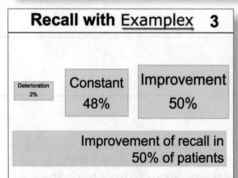

This diagram is another example of enhanced layout and design. The surface area of the three squares is weighted according to the relative importance of the group. Form and colour are reminiscent of Post-it® Notes. A similar version to the example was chosen by the company advertising Climodien®.

Make your diagrams clear

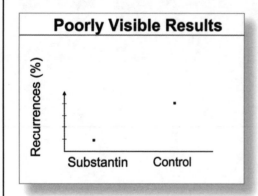

Consider the following results of a clinical trial in herpes virus infections: Substantin reduced recurrences by 75%. Imagine you are sent the diagram shown in the chart.

What is your first impression? This version has a number of elements that you might improve to represent the results more persuasively.

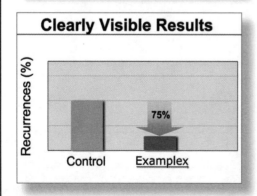

Dots have been replaced by columns. The product column has been moved to the right-hand side. An arrow indicates movement and highlights the product benefit. A relevant number has been added. The typed substance name has been replaced by the product logo. (In scientific documents, you would of course retain the substance name rather than the brand name.)

Use your brand colour

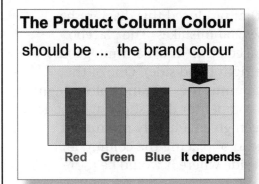

Always use your brand colour for the column depicting your product. If your brand colour is red, then the column should be in red. If your brand colour is blue, then the column should be in blue. Don't let your agency get away with a different colour.

Your readers should associate the colour and the data set with your brand. This helps them to recognize at once which results belong to your product.

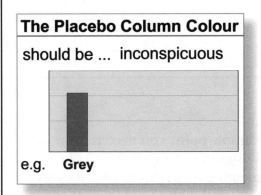

Use a design for the column or pie chart segment representing the placebo or control group that ensures clear differentiation from the comparator. The obvious choice is the use of the colour grey in its various shades. This makes the placebo column unobtrusive.

Use contrasting colours

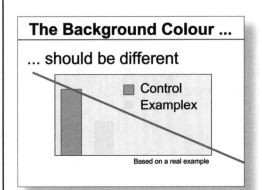

Choose a background colour that ensures sufficient contrast. Avoid using a shade of the brand colour which may only confuse the brand and control drugs.

Beware of the design pitfalls

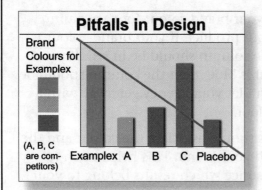

The agency that produced this diagram has committed several mistakes. The placebo column is placed at the most advantageous position (the right hand side). One of the competitor columns uses a brand colour (light brown). The competitor data showing superior results has been given a highly prominent position instead of placing the column at the left hand side where it would be more appropriate.

Think 'black and white'

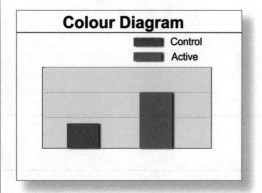

There is one simple point you need to bear in mind when designing or approving a colour diagram. Remember that sales representatives may make black-and-white photocopies or may fax your colour diagram (which will then invariably come out in black-and-white).

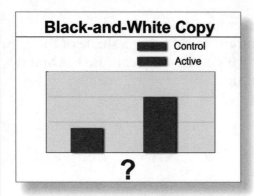

In this example, the reader cannot distinguish which column represents which group, since the blue and green chosen as original colours became virtually indistinguishable when transformed into greyscale.

Label columns directly

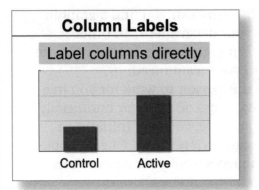

Avoid using keys in diagrams (which is often the default choice in your computer software). Label the columns directly instead. This allows the product column to be easily identified even on a black-and-white copy.

Test your colour illustrations

Checking for Photocopies

Before approving a colour document, make a black-and-white copy

Before giving your approval to any colour document, make a black-and-white print-out or a black-and-white photocopy and check that it is clearly understandable.

Work on your design skills

A Graphic Designer

Designer

Invite someone to your team who has experience in designing graphics, posters, ads and other types of visual communication

Look around: Where can you find a graphic designer? In your department? In other departments? In your external agency? Invite this person to your team meetings.

Can you get this person to work for you in a more intensive way - officially or unofficially? If this is not possible, consider initiating a 'style and design review board' where people comment on pieces from your competitors as well as on your own internal drafts.

DEVISING DIRECT MAIL THAT GETS GOOD RESPONSES

Open a dialogue with your customers

Customer Dialogue

My answer

'Talk' and 'listen' to your customers by direct-response marketing

If you incorporate a response element into your communication activities, for example email, regular mailings, or advertising, you are inviting a dialogue with your customers. There are communication agencies that specialize in direct-response marketing. Use them.

Target the recipient

Targeting the Recipient

You as healthcare professional

You as a physician

You as an internist

You as a cardiologist

The more precise, the better

Be as specific as you can when addressing your prospect. This example illustrates how you can improve your targeting of a cardiologist. If a doctor specializes in an area of medicine, make sure your address reflects their specialization. Use any data from mailing responses (for example the card they stamped) to improve the accuracy of your database.

Find credible gatekeepers

Relationship Marketing

FAX INFO

In Cooperation with the Society for ....

Hormonal Contraception in Patients with Diabetes mellitus

....
....

A Scientific Service
from Company ABC   **Examplex**

Ask a professional medical society if they are willing to cooperate with you in providing scientific information to physicians as part of the process of continuing medical education. You will need to select a topic and title relevant to your study and to your target group. In this instance, the look and feel of the fax should be neutral, scientific and research-oriented. It should not give the impression of a promotional flyer or folder. Your branding should be subtle.

Use suggestive design

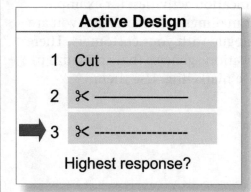

You offer free article reprints or brochures? Then you want the physician to fill out the coupon, cut it out and send it to you. Based on direct marketing experience, version 1 will give you the lowest response rate, whereas version 3 will give you the highest response rate. Sometimes the simplest aspect of design can have a big impact on response rates.

Trade on familiarity

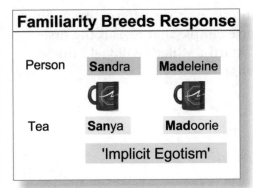

Maurice Carvallo and his colleagues at the State University in New York were responsible for an enlightening experiment. They asked participants to sample two cups of tea. The first three letters in the name of one of the teas were devised to match the first three letters in participants' first names. When asked to choose one of the teas to take home as gift, participants preferred the tea that contained the letters of their name.

We value what looks familiar. The more the elements of your communication (words, symbols and images) reflect an environment that the doctor is familiar with, the more likely she or he will connect with what you have to say. Use the vocabulary and visuals with which the doctor is familiar and feels comfortable. This form of implicit self-interest acts below the level of our conscious awareness and may be more persuasive than more obvious strategies.

Personalize your letters

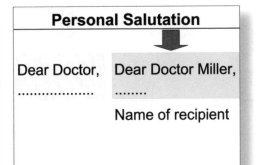

Make your letter as personal as possible. Use the recipient's name in the salutation of your letter. 'Dear Doctor Miller' will elicit more response than just 'Dear Doctor'.

Disclose your first name

The illustration shows three alternative endings to a letter. The example that reveals the first name (using 'Martin Miller') will yield the highest response.

Avoid ostentatious signatures

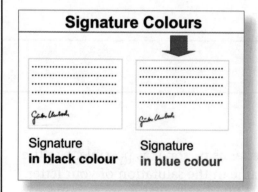

A mailing will yield a higher response when the signatures are printed in blue rather than black. And don't be tempted to try any more unusual or flashy colours such as red or green.

Enclose your business card

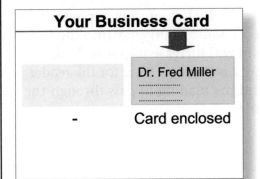

If you are sending a small mailing (200 to 300 or letters or less), consider enclosing your business card with the letter. Many people will look at the business card (so make sure that it also displays the name of your product) and whilst they will throw away the letter, some of them will keep the business card.

Show the incentive

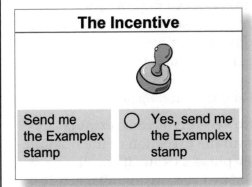

'Yes, send me the Examplex stamp' affirms positive action, includes a 'yes' and thus will secure a higher response rate than simply 'Send me the Examplex stamp'. Include an illustration or incentive in your letter so that the recipient can see what he or she will receive: a stamp, a CD, a reprinted article, and so on. Always show clearly what you are offering. Be sure to observe promotional codes when sending out material.

Create a sense of urgency

The Power of Deadlines

31
July

This offer expires 31 July
So mail the reply card today

State the date by which your offer expires. This will inject a sense of urgency into the promotion and will increase response. Make sure you allow a reasonable time for the reader to respond and the mailing to pass through the postal system.

Test and test again

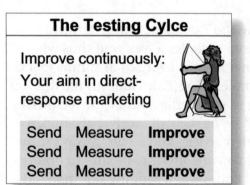

The Testing Cylce

Improve continuously:
Your aim in direct-response marketing

Send	Measure	**Improve**
Send	Measure	**Improve**
Send	Measure	**Improve**

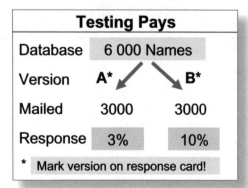

Testing Pays

Database	6 000 Names	
Version	A*	B*
Mailed	3000	3000
Response	3%	10%

* Mark version on response card!

Think about how you can improve the effectiveness of your mailings. Use the methods of direct response marketing:
send, measure, improve and then restart the cycle.
Test, improve and then test again!

- develop two versions of your text, that are identical with the exception of the headline or some key phrases (Note: If you can't send out the two versions simultaneously, consider sending them one after the other);
- select the sample list of doctors in the data base;
- split the doctors into two random groups ('randomize them');
- mark the two versions appropriately, so you can identify which version of the mailing they received when they do respond (for example 'A' or 'B' on the reply card);
- send out the mailing;
- measure the response for each version.

In this example, version 'B' is obviously more effective than version 'A'. Continue testing and improving version 'B' to increase your response rates further. Find out which headlines or key words work best for you!

Always measure the response to your activities

Response Measurement

Measure and Adjust

Record the customers' response to every activity

Then improve it

Try to add a direct response element to every marketing activity you undertake.

Record the response. Since you have objective and precise quantitative feedback from your customers, you can easily adjust and improve your previous versions.

USING IMAGES AND ILLUSTRATIONS

Know the advantage of visual information

The Speed of Thought

Speak	**150**	
Speak	Spoken language	
Think	**600**	
Think	'Mental language stream'	

Speed (Words per minute)

We can think about four times faster than we can speak. Our minds move faster than our lips. While you are talking, the listener has time to think about other things. Give them some visual information reinforcing your message as you speak to help them better focus on what you are trying to say.

Use visual information

The Impact of Images

Visual information

works at a subconscious level

is less analyzed than words

is stored more efficiently than text

Images and illustrations tend to be less analyzed than spoken or written words and are generally more memorable. Images work beneath our 'intellectual radar' and can influence the subconscious mind more readily than words.

The words you utter will be rapidly forgotten, but illustrations often have a lasting impact.

Choose the right symbol

The Right Triangle

Which product seems more effective in **lowering** cholesterol?

CRES▼   CRES▲

The illustration shows two versions of a triangle: One pointing downwards and one pointing upwards. If you want your symbol to indicate that your product decreases something such as blood levels of a certain substance, you naturally choose the triangle pointing downwards.

If on the other hand you want your symbol to indicate that your product increases something, then you would of course choose the triangle pointing upwards.

Visualize your message

Appropriate Images

Picture

Illustration

Symbol

Icon

Choose a visual or metaphor relevant to your message

Close your eyes and imagine the picture, symbol, icon or metaphor that could illustrate your message. An appropriate visual helps to get your prospect's mind thinking in the right direction. And it helps to focus them on the right theme. Test your choice with colleagues and selected customers to make sure they readily identify the link between image and message.

Night and Day

A simple example that uses common symbols for the sun and the moon to highlight the efficacy of the product during 24 hours.

Visualize your message (cont)

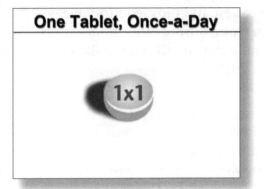

One Tablet, Once-a-Day

The picture of the tablet and the numbers '1x1' illustrate convincingly the convenience of the easy once-daily dosing schedule.

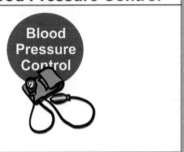

Blood Pressure Control

The image of a blood pressure monitor will be recognized by doctors and patients alike and serves to illustrate effective blood pressure control.

Suitable for Young Women

Red roses

Convenient Contraception

See also   www.laralove.de and www.laralove.ch

The image of red roses is used by one company to illustrate that one of the contraceptive pills it is marketing is especially suitable for young women. The names of the websites for this product, 'laralove.de' and 'laralove.ch' are in line with the chosen symbol.

Make use of all your image sources

Images on the Web

A great source of new ideas:
Type a keyword and let a
search engine (*Google*) find
• suitable words
• suitable pictures

www.inmagine.com
www.agefotostock.com

What is the easiest and most comfortable way to get design clues, during office hours at no charge to your company (if it has a flat rate for access to the internet)?
The answer: let the web inspire you.

Make use of search engines (such as Google) to help you to find appropriate words and images. Just type in a keyword and let the search engine do the work for you. There are also various image data banks. However be aware of copyright. Make sure you are clear what you may use at no charge and what you will need permission for. Do not compromise the impact of your message by using a free image that is not appropriate simply because it is free.

Employ colour for images

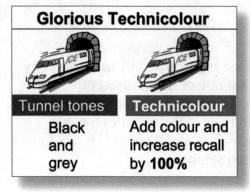

Colour images increase recall by around 100 per cent compared to their black-and-white equivalents. Insist on colour even if your advertising agency tells you that a black-and-white image is more 'creative'.

'Humanize' your pieces

People Pictures

'Humanize' your piece with pictures of human beings

Easy intravenous application

People are always interested in people. 'Humanize' your folders, advertisements, brochures and so on with pictures of people.

Prefer photographs to illustrations

Art Work or Photographs

Paintings, Drawings

Abstract
Hypothetical
Creative

Photographs

Authentic
Genuine
True

Photographs appear more authentic than artists' illustrations. Photographs, as a result, have a bigger impact. Therefore move from abstract art work to photographs.

Always make sure that any photographs you use support your message. Check copyright before use.

Pay for professional photography

Professional Photography

	Lends credibility to your promotion
Good photos	Do not try to save money with poor photos

Spend some of your budget on an excellent potographer

Good photography has enormous value and will make your promotion more credible. Trying to save money with cheaper photography is a false economy. Do not use pictures from one of the commercially available image data bases. Instead find yourself a good photographer and invest in high-quality photos. Explain which mood, atmosphere and concept the picture needs to convey. Adapt the colour of the background or of certain objects within the photo so that they exactly match the colour of your brand.

Show the package

Showing What You Sell

Which picture works best?

Tablet   Blister   Package

Packshot

Use a picture of your package ('packshot') in your advertisements and folders. Since many doctors do not know what your package looks like, a packshot will familiarize them with the appearance of the product.

Samples often go straight from the reception to the patient without the doctor ever seeing them. If you show your product on every folder, brochure and other document you'll encourage the doctor to recognize your product. I would therefore ask my advertising agency to meet my requirements, although this is a matter for debate amongst marketers.

CREATING EMOTIONAL IMPACT

Distinguish between the value and impact of data

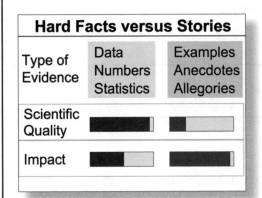

Hard Facts versus Stories

Type of Evidence	Data Numbers Statistics	Examples Anecdotes Allegories
Scientific Quality		
Impact		

Hard data, numbers and statistics ('just the facts'), have a high scientific value. Soft data, examples, anecdotes and allegories, have a high emotional value ('just stories'). A study of 23 000 US consumers has shown that emotions have twice as much influence on the buying decision as pure information. The impact of emotionally moving material is much greater than the impact of 'hard data'. Doctors themselves are influenced by the emotional aspects of your message as well as by the numbers. Therefore, give them both.

Build an emotional bond

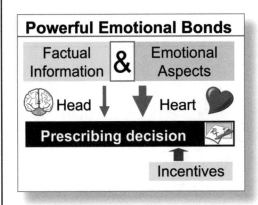

Powerful Emotional Bonds

Factual Information **&** Emotional Aspects

Head ↓ ↓ Heart

Prescribing decision

↑ Incentives

Link the hard data – the scientific results – from your trial to the emotional aspects of the disease and treatment. You need to reach the readers' minds as well as their hearts.

Telling a human interest story is an obvious method for making this link and addressing people's emotions.

Tell a captivating human interest story

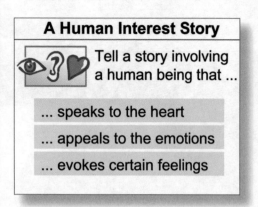

People are interested in people. All of us have a natural curiosity about other people. The human interest approach, which tells stories about people, is a proven advertising technique to make your product more exciting and to increase the number of people who see, watch, and actually read your ads, folders and letters.

Imagine a concept that places your product at the centre of a human drama. In medicine, this is the 'typical patient' or 'clinical case'. There is no need to be a novelist or screenwriter. There are enough patient records from the clinical trial to provide you with the raw material for your story. This approach gives vivid examples to the doctors and can serve to facilitate diagnosis and treatment of appropriate patients.

Use evidence-based arguments

Evidence Based on Numbers

Real Economic Value

Cost control and savings in antihypertensive therapy

Compared to major competitor: Savings of $111 a year

Examplex
10 mg

The statements in this illustration are straightforward (and boring). The message of 'real economic value' is supported by logical, rational arguments to prove the claim of 'value for money'.

Combine facts and feelings

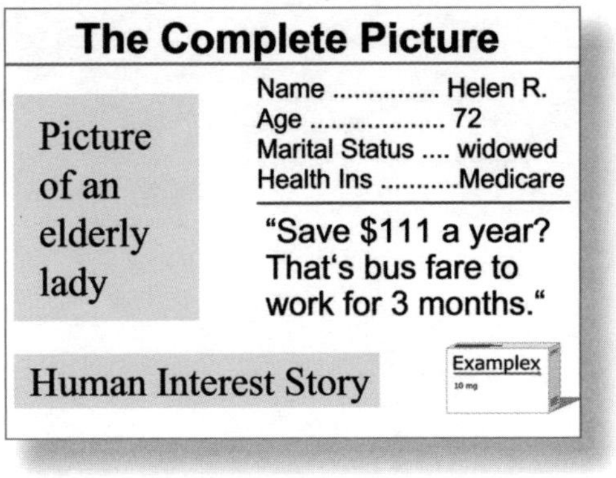

The Complete Picture

Picture
of an
elderly
lady

Name .... Helen R.
Age 72
Marital Status .... widowed
Health Ins ....Medicare

"Save $111 a year?
That's bus fare to
work for 3 months."

Human Interest Story

Examplex
10 mg

In this illustration we are introduced to a real person: We know her first name, her age, her marital status and her health insurance details. The figure of $111 now becomes the very tangible and imaginable 'bus fare to work for 3 months'. A similar campaign was successfully used by Bayer Corporation to market Adalat®CC (long-acting nifedipine) in the United States.

IMPROVING YOUR BRANDING SKILLS

Remember the hallmarks of successful brands

Hallmarks of Branding	
Competence	Solve a problem
Credibility	Be honest
Concentration	Remain focused
Continuity	Be consistent

Think of the 4 'C's:

- **Competence**
  Show relevance to physicians' and patients' needs and solve a particular problem
- **Credibility**
  Evoke trust by being honest about the risk-benefit ratio
- **Concentration**
  Get a clear focus and limit your communication to the essentials
- **Continuity**
  Keep up consistency over time.

Build a 'lighthouse' identity

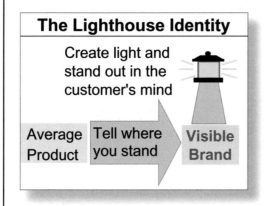

The Lighthouse Identity

Create light and stand out in the customer's mind

Average Product → Tell where you stand → Visible Brand

If you want to sharpen your brand's profile you need make it clear what you stand for and what you don't stand for. Only then do you have a chance that your brand will become a trusted trade mark for your customers. Ask yourself:

- what sort of identity – what sort of personality – does our brand have?
- what does our brand stand for?
- what is the fundamental brand promise?

Align your marketing activities

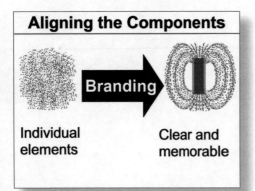

Aligning the Components

Individual elements → Branding → Clear and memorable

Many products fail to achieve a tangible identity in the customer's mind because the marketing activities associated with them are fragmented. It is easy to spend money on various promotional activities, but without a clear overall branding concept their effect is similar to a powerboat without a rudder.

Branding provides direction and helps you to line up the individual elements of your communication strategy so that all of your activities move you in the same direction.

Use your brand identity

The Role of the Brand

Examplex 10 mg — The brand's

unique identity

distinctive character

special look and feel

can help market your trial

Use the brand to facilitate the marketing of your trial results. If you connect brand and the trial closely, they can reinforce and enhance one another. There are hidden synergies between your brand and your trial that can strengthen your brand. Discover them. Exploit them.

Build brand equity

Brand Equity	
The new trial can	
Re-energize	
Re-vitalize	Examplex 10 mg
Re-juvenate	your brand
Build more brand equity	

Use the trial results to re-energize, re-vitalize and rejuvenate your brand. The brand exposure associated with the communication of the trial results can help you strengthen the value of your brand.

Brand all your material

The Complete Brand Identity	
Name	Visuals / Design
Logo	Style
Message	Symbols
Vocabulary	Colours
	Photos
Check branding guidelines Ensure consistency	

Remember to pay attention to all the characteristics that describe a brand: Name, logo, message, vocabulary, visuals and so on. These elements, 'the look, feel and touch' of the brand, will determine how your customers feel about your product. If any of these elements are unclear or confused, you need to clarify them immediately.

Brand your emails

Your Email Identity

Best regards,
Joe Smith

Suggested Signatures

Product Manager Examplex

Examplex Marketing Team

Coordinator Examplex ABC Communication

The email auto-signature is the text block that your software automatically inserts at the end of every email you write. Make sure that your electronic auto-signature, along with the auto-signatures of your team, mentions your brand. Many emails I receive from marketers, mention the company and the department, but fail to mention the brand – big mistake! The same applies to printed correspondence. Don't miss this opportunity.

Exploit the mathematics of emails

The Mathematics of Emails

	20	emails per day
x	200	working days
=	4 000	product messages sent

Automatic promotion with
no additional cost

If you have a (short and not too overtly promotional) message you wish to spread far and wide, your email auto-signature is a good place for it. The illustration gives an example: If you send 20 emails per day and you work 200 days of the year, you will send out 4 000 emails with the product message - free of charge.

Learn from branding failures and successes

Failed Branding

Slide Kit

The ABC Trial

Slide kit with study results,
based on a real example

This illustration is based on a real example. 'The slide kit displayed 'Slide Kit' in large letters and the name of the trial in smaller print. Neither message, disease, substance, nor brand were mentioned. The product managers that paid the agency to produce this piece clearly wasted their money.

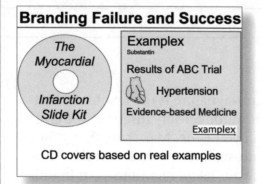

Branding Failure and Success

The Myocardial

Infarction Slide Kit

Examplex
Substantin

Results of ABC Trial

Hypertension

Evidence-based Medicine

Examplex

CD covers based on real examples

The left-hand CD containing study results illustrates a real-world example of what you should not do - produce a CD that only mentions the disease, but fails to mention the brand name or at least the chemical substance name in a style and colour that reminds the reader of the brand. Nor does it contain a symbol or logo or photo that would remind the viewer of the brand - a clear failure in branding.

The right-hand CD illustrates a much more successful example: brand name, substance name, trial name, a symbol, the disease, a competitive advantage and the product logo are all clearly visible. A CD cover similar to this was produced by AstraZeneca for a compendium of key clinical studies investigating its combination antihypertensive product, Zestoretic®.

Remember: change is bad news

Temptation to Change

from your Advertising Agency:

We have great creative ideas ... we will make it more modern.

We want to produce a new expensive campaign!

If your advertising agency calls you and suggests that you update or rejuvenate your campaign, beware. They may promise 'We will make it more modern' or 'We will make it look fresh'. Of course this campaign will bring in more money – for the agency. Remember the old brand advice 'Every change is poison for the long-term success of the brand!' Resist the temptation and practise a 'hands-off' attitude.

Ensure branding consistency

Consistency

Provide a single consistent voice to the outside world

Play it again, Sam

Stick to the same piece

You need to sustain the same look for your brand in all your materials and events. Practise consistency. Stick to the same proven familiar appearance. Enforce adherence to branding guidelines. Remember 'Brand work is boring work'.

ADAPTING TO A PROFESSIONAL ROLE

The way you communicate plays a pivotal role in the success of the project. Personally communicating a message is more effective and more memorable than is possible through the printed word and the printed image. A study on communication concluded that we convey only approximately seven per cent of our feelings and attitudes through the use of words. Thus we convey approximately 93 per cent of our likes and dislikes through non-verbal means. This emphasizes the importance of your voice (volume, tone, pitch) and of your body language (gestures, eye contact) which can be more important than your words.

Use the techniques in this section to help you maintain a high profile through personal communication:

- engage yourself!
- speak to people!
- give presentations!

Train your voice

Learning to Speak
Speak loudly
Articulate clearly and pronounce precisely
Develop tone and pitch of your voice

Train your voice by speaking out loud. Articulate clearly, pronounce words precisely. Develop tone and pitch of your voice. Consider taking lessons from a speech coach.

Remember that the gap between your words can also convey your message.

You need to be aware of your intonation and the speed at which you are speaking.

Sharpen your presentation skills

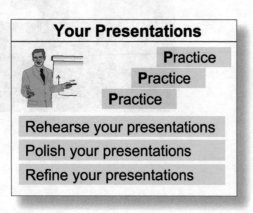

Practise your presentation skills whenever you have the opportunity.

Rehearse them, polish them, refine them – continuously.

Practise your presentations in front of a mirror or better yet: have them videotaped and review them later.

Pay as much attention to your non-verbal signals (volume, tone and pitch of your voice as well as body language) as you do to the words themselves.

Become a top performer

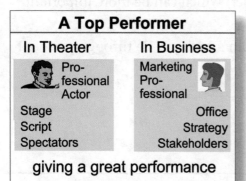

There are similarities between the theatre and business; there is drama in both. You are a marketing professional realising a strategy in a work place, usually your office or a company conference room. You don't only have passive spectators, but you also have active stakeholders whom you wish to engage.

Professional actors as well as professional marketers give the world a great performance. Imagine yourself on stage and become a top performer.

Consider the company as your theatre

The Company Stage

Theatre: It's show time

The curtain opens: You're on!

You may find a particular frame of mind useful to put you more at ease during presentations. You are the boss of your own show that is currently playing at a theatre bearing the name of your company. This is the setting for your performance. Set the stage. Think of the company as your stage and see yourself as a performing actor on that stage. This state of mind will help you to relax and to give more persuasive presentations. But remember, the best actors know not to overact. Showmanship is no substitute for intimate knowledge of the market and the product.

Learn to connect with your audience

Audience Rapport

Reach out

Relate to people

Connect with people

Don't think of a presentation as a monologue. You are not lecturing people. Presentations are designed to influence people and win friends. Reach out to the audience. Try to get on their wave length. Relate to them as fellow professionals. Connect with them. Ask them questions. Listen to their comments. Appreciate their contributions. Show that you care about them. In short, establish rapport on a human level.

Cultivate your sense of humour

Humour	
Have fun	
Relax	**Take office life easier**
	Look for comic aspects
Smile and laugh more often	

Make liberal use of the one universally recognized communication that only mankind is capable of: laughter and smiles. Humour can help establish instant rapport with other human beings. You can cultivate your sense of humour, especially about yourself.

If this sounds like bitter medicine, nevertheless you need to take it. People who show a sense of humour are usually more successful in business than people who never smile.

BECOMING MORE RESOURCEFUL

What you do is important. What you do matters. Your aim is to put your project clearly on the company map, to put it at the top of the list of projects. How do you transform your project into a high priority project ? You start by working with what you have, with where you are. Necessity is the mother of invention. Use the techniques in this section to help you spell out what you need and get it.

Communicate your project

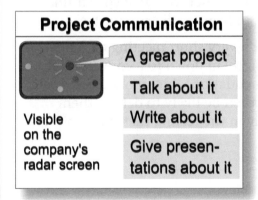

Project Communication

A great project

Talk about it

Write about it

Give presentations about it

Visible on the company's radar screen

You need to sell your project internally.

Talk about your project, write about your project, give presentations about your project! Sell the study as a golden business opportunity - one that should not be missed. Make it clear to the internal stakeholders that your project:

- will strengthen the company's competitive advantage
- will add commercial value
- will help the company win in the market place.

Try to avoid formal 'steering committees' or 'advisory boards'; you won't be able to control them and they can actually slow you down.

Ensure sufficient resources

You need to secure adequate resources in your company. Without enough resources, your plans are doomed from the start. Think big when you are assessing the money and people needed to implement your project. Remember to plan for contingencies. Don't be tempted to cut financial corners. Remember 'Better to ask for too much than for too little'.

You may find a particular frame of mind useful when asking for sufficient resources. Consider yourself going on a fundraising drive to generate appropriate funds for your team.

Seek out support from key persons

Good Cover	
I support it	**Before** a formal presentation
	Before asking for approval
Endorsement from key persons	**Before** a decision is made
The project should be their baby	

Before seeking official approval, try to build informal acceptance or consent from influential key players in your organization (for example from selected senior executives or members of top management). Early personal buy-in from the top of the organization will increase the likelihood of getting a subsequent positive decision when you give your formal presentation in front of the committee.

Ask them for a very short meeting on a one-to-one basis. Pin them down to a conversation. Ask them for their advice. Try to follow their recommendations. Incorporate their suggestions into your presentation because they will then be likely to defend them during the meeting when questioned. Give each of them the feeling that this project is also 'their baby'.

Play the numbers game

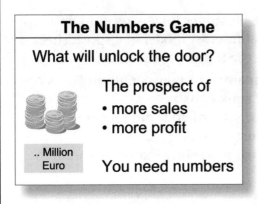

Fundraising time! What is it that unlocks the door to the decision makers? What gets you over the tough hurdle of securing additional resources? The prospect of more sales and more profit. You need to play the numbers game. Take time to develop your mathematical forecast model, then test it using various sets of assumptions and numbers until you have perfected it. Talk to the controllers in the finance department to make sure that your figures have covered all bases.

Leverage the investment in clinical development

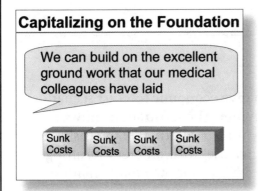

Remember that past trial costs do not enter into your financial equation. These 'sunk costs' can never be recovered and therefore have no influence on the actual decision (contrary to the opinion some people in your organization may have). So, when you estimate the commercial value of your project, be sure that these sunk costs do not enter your mathematical forecast model. Run your financial model on future costs only.

You may wish to acknowledge that you can capitalize on the solid foundations that your colleagues in the clinical development department have constructed. This groundwork is made up of the contacts the clinical development teams have established with the investigators, patient advocacy groups, opinion leaders, scientific societies, and so on. Their network will prove very valuable in your marketing activities. Thus, you are cashing in on the investments that your company has already made.

Spell out your assumptions

Your Assumptions

- Company spent 5 million Euro on the trial
- Annual product sales are 10 million Euro
- Your Marketing Budget is 1 million Euro

Your estimate: With an additional 1 million Euro for one year in your Marketing Budget you could improve sales by
- 20% during the first year and by
- 10% during the second year

Worthwhile investment?

The example illustrates how you could develop your financial forecast model in a spreadsheet. Let's assume the following numbers:

- your company has spent 5 million Euros on the trial ('sunk costs')
- the annual sales of your product are 10 million Euros
- your annual marketing budget is 1 million Euros.

You estimate that – with an additional one million Euros for one year in your marketing budget – you will improve sales by 20% during the first year and by 10% during the second year.

The question: how can you back up your claims and show that the additional investment will indeed be worthwhile?

Develop comparative scenarios

Comparative Scenarios (Mill Euro)

I Same	2006	2007	Sum
Marketing Budget	1	1	2
Revenue Forecast	10	10	20

II Increase	2006	2007	Sum
Marketing Budget	2	1	3
Revenue Forecast	12	11	23

Increase revenue by 20% in 1st and by 10% in 2nd year

Create alternative economic forecast scenarios on your computer. The illustration shows a spreadsheet with two alternative forecasts called 'same' and 'increase' with different resulting outcomes. Develop your own mathematical model in an electronic spreadsheet. Choose your criteria and lay out the pertinent numbers in rows and columns. Run the model with various numbers to see what sort of output results you generate for the bottom line.

Highlight the project's commercial value

The Right Conclusion

Increase marketing budget by **1 million Euro**
and increase revenue by **3 million Euro**

=

By spending an additional **1 million Euro**
you get additional sales of **3 million Euro**

Certainly a worthwhile investment!

The project is worth funding

Increasing the marketing budget by one million Euros results in a three million Euro increase in revenue. In other words, in this example, spending an additional one million Euros yields additional sales of three million Euros. (Note: the increase in variable costs, for example production, is considered negligible). Thus you demonstrate the project's profit potential. The conclusion that the increase in the marketing budget would be a worthwhile investment, is compelling.

Ask for the budget

Asking for the Budget

One million Euro

A worthwhile investment

Ask for the money

Your project is worth it

Go for it

Ask for the full resources you need. Be courageous and ask for the money. Your project is worth it. Avoid the risk of getting an inappropriately low budget approved, only to exceed your expenses later on. Ensure an adequate budget for your activities before you start.

This approach avoids the unpleasant situation whereby your boss asks you a year later 'Then, why didn't you ask for more money?'

Use your budget

Spending the Money	
Controllers	Once the budget is approved, spend it!
	Beware a subsequent budget cut

Once your budget is approved, be ready to spend it. Or at least to allocate it firmly.

Beware a subsequent budget cut that may claw back resources and compromise your marketing activities.

So prevent the controllers from taking your money away.

MARKETING INTERNALLY

Marketing clinical trial results involves internal politics. If you succeed, you will invariably change the status quo and thus invade someone's turf. You will meet internal resistance from risk-averse control fanatics and procedure-loving bureaucrats in your organization. Use the ideas in this section to build an ingenious internal marketing programme that will help you meet these challenges.

Develop an internal marketing programme

The Internal Strategy

Your internal marketing programme clears road blocks in the company

Remove (invisible) barriers

The internal marketing programme is designed to skilfully overcome internal obstacles.
You need to enlist broad support within the company. You need to ensure word-of-mouth marketing for your project.

Adopt a pragmatic attitude: be candid and frank, but at the same time astute, so you can navigate towards your goal.

Focus on overt and implicit messages

Your Overt Message

Waking people up

The project: A golden business opportunity	
The strategy for capturing that opportunity	
Winning in the market place	

The overt message on which you focus should be:

The clinical trial is a golden business opportunity we should take advantage of.

The team has designed a conclusive strategy for exploiting that opportunity.

The team can help the company to win in the market place.

Wake people up to a fantastic commercial opportunity.

Show them how your project will add value.

Your Implicit Message

The ideal person for making the most of it

You

The internal marketing programme is also your internal personal recognition programme

The message hidden beneath the overt message is: You are the person with the solution for taking advantage of this commercial opportunity. You are the appropriate person to steer the project - officially or unofficially. You are the ideal candidate to take charge of this project. So your internal marketing programme is as much about marketing you as it is about marketing the trial.

Enlarge your network of supporters

Expanding Your Network

Search the organization for supporters

Cast your net widely   Find allies

You will need allies in the organization. Potential supporters and friends can be found in all sorts of different places - some close at hand, others further away. Look for them near and far. Cast your net widely. Try to reach as many people as possible.

Keep selected senior managers in the loop by setting up brief personal meetings with them or by sending them personalized emails about the progress you are making. If you do this diligently, you should be able to obtain support from the 'establishment' in your organization.

Sell the project inside your company first

Internal Marketing Programme

Activities inside your organi- zation	Meetings with top management
	Internal presentations
	Internal publications
	Internal interviews
	Intranet
	Communication platform
	Incorporate the sales force
	Get support from headquarters
	Inform all stakeholders

Just as you plan and direct an external marketing campaign aimed at your external customers, so you need to plan and direct an internal marketing campaign aimed at your internal customers. Make sure you feel comfortable about selling your project internally. The illustration offers an overview of possible activities.

Involve decision makers

The Role of Decision Makers

The bottleneck is at the top of the bottle

Senior management

Give VIP treatment to key players

Take the time to enlist support from senior management. Remember: the bottleneck is usually at the top of the bottle and not at the bottom. Direct some attention to the top management in your organization. Give the 'Very Important Persons' a VIP treatment.

Enlist support from senior management

Help from Top Management

Set up face-to-face meetings with senior executives

Advice from the top

Ask for one-to-one discussions

Seek their suggestions

Incorporate their recommendations

Here are a few tips when asking for support:

- be clear and concise
- listen actively
- ask people for their advice
- show your appreciation for their contributions and their time.

Give frequent presentations

Presenting Your Project

| Present repeatedly | Use every opportunity to promote your project |

Use every appropriate opportunity to promote your project. Deliver short persuasive presentations at:

- department meetings
- workshops
- committees
- other events.

Always emphasize the value for the company.

Place articles in internal newsletters

Internal Publications

Company Newsletter
1 July 2006

Impressive Results
......
......

Produced by
- Corporate
- Business Unit
- Department

Appoint a coordinator for in-house promotion

Look for regular coverage of your project in the company newsletter during the implementation phase of your project. The editors of these publications are usually happy to receive articles and are grateful for interesting and uplifting stories (in a ready-to-use electronic format).

Who in your team could volunteer to coordinate this in-house promotion?

Initiate internal interviews

The Big Internal Interview
Ask the right questions
Record it
Choose an experienced journalist
Brief the journalist
Brief the CEO

The top person on the ladder has enormous influence. If you are working in a smaller company where you have frequent contact with your top managers, you can quote them in discussions and presentations. However, if you are working in a large company where you have little direct contact with top managers, consider setting up an interview with your Chief Executive Officer or Chairperson. Remember to check with your own boss first. Use an experienced journalist or reporter to ask the right questions. This can be someone from your company's communication department or from your public relations agency.

Brief both the CEO and the journalist. The journalist needs to know the answers that will be useful to you. It is then up to him or her to formulate the appropriate questions.

Ask the right questions

The Right Question	
Is this study important?	Why is this study so important?
	⬆

The illustration gives an example of open questions that increase the probability that you will get the answers you want. Instead of asking 'Is this study important to you?' the reporter should ask 'Why is this study so important to you?'

Instead of asking 'Have you got the resources to communicate these results?' the reporter might ask 'How can you ensure that these results are effectively communicated?'

On the day of the interview make sure you record the interview with a digital camera. This provides the basis for 'recycling' various segments of the interview on digital media, such as the intranet.

Exploit the heirarchy

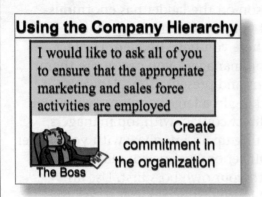

CEOs generally want to emphasize their company's (and their own) importance. They know that their statements will be used only for internal company purposes. Consequently their answers will be positive and uplifting. In one case the president of one major pharmaceutical company was sceptical about committing substantial resources to the marketing campaign for a particular trial. During the interview, however, he replied to one question with the statement 'I would like to ask all of you to ensure that the appropriate marketing and sales force activities take place.' You might select a similar scene from your digital video recording of the interview, store it on your laptop and use this 'video clip' to introduce your presentations. Sharing this statement from the boss with stakeholders in the company very much helps to enlist support and create commitment.

Develop your intranet site

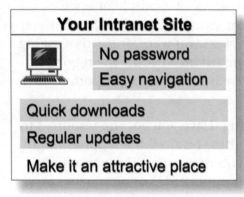

Think of your intranet site as a living document. Make it an attractive place to visit. Your goal is to encourage people to see it as a toolbox where they can find up-to-date information.

Some tips to this end:

- avoid barriers such as passwords, which people tend to forget
- make navigation as easy as possible
- only put short documents on the site so that they are quick to download
- use easy-to-use formats so people can benefit directly in their daily work
- update your site regularly and remove outdated documents
- include a 'search site' service function
- include a site map linking the various terms with the respective pages.

A word of caution: Avoid the common mistake of putting huge documents (of several megabytes) onto the site. These require a lengthy downloading and people will be unlikely to bother.

Use the intranet to save time

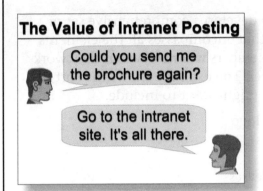

The Value of Intranet Posting

Could you send me the brochure again?

Go to the intranet site. It's all there.

You and your assistants may well spend time answering requests from colleagues. They ask you for a brochure or a questions-and-answers list. If you put this kind of material in the intranet, you'll find it easier and less time consuming to guide your colleagues there rather than needing to search for the file in the directory of your computer and then having to email the file personally. Take advantage of the intranet and ease your work load.

Write emails with hyperlinks

Email Hyperlinks

Send regular emails with electronic links to your intranet

The study shows exciting results, since Examplex clearly improved ... ⇒ **more**

Increase traffic to your site

Make full use of your emails to guide readers to your intranet. Send regular emails that contain statements that are electronically linked to your internal site.

For example: 'The study showed some exciting results, since Examplex was able to improve the outcome of ... ' followed by a hyperlink. A simple click then links the reader directly to the pertinent page of your intranet site which will increase traffic to your site.

Two things to remember when writing this kind of email:

- keep it short
- spell out the benefit to the reader.

Build a complete communication platform

Communication Platform

Content
- Product logo
- Diagrams
- Pictures
- Press releases
- Publications
- Questions & Answers

Database with all elements for product promotion

Take time to develop a comprehensive set of documents that encompasses all the elements your team members will need when they work on the project. The example shows the sort of content you might want to include:

- product logo
- diagrams
- pictures
- press releases
- publications
- questions & answers.

Try 'questions-and-answers'

The Q & A Section

People like
Questions & Answers

Question
Why is this study important?

Answer
This is the first study that ...

Research has shown that 'questions and answers' is an excellent format for encouraging readers to read text. You need to think carefully to craft the kind of questions that will generate the answers you wish to communicate.

Test your draft 'Q & A' section extensively before you put it into your final document.

Produce electronic and hard copy versions

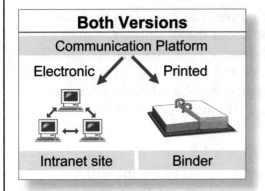

Make sure you prepare both electronic and printed versions of your communication platform. The existence of a physical version highlights the importance of your project and gives it a tangible reality that is not there with the purely electronic version.

Exploit the magic of the printed word. Most people will welcome a nice binder with an attractive cover carrying the brand logo and the name of the trial.

Educate the sales representatives

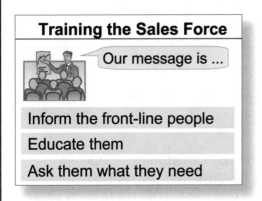

Your sales force is the most effective and also the most expensive way to promote your product. Establish close links with the sales representatives. Effective cooperation with them is the key to driving sales. Try to attend as many national or regional sales force meetings as your schedule allows. Communicate with the field force on a regular basis. Make sure you are available to explain the marketing strategy, the message, the marketing pieces your team has developed. Emphasize the importance of branding. You may feel as if you are preaching to the choir, but stick with it.

These sales meetings offer you an additional bonus - unfiltered feedback from front-line people. Ask them what they need in order to use the study results more effectively to support the clinical use of the product. They will tell you. Use their suggestions to fine-tune your marketing strategy.

Check the incentives scheme

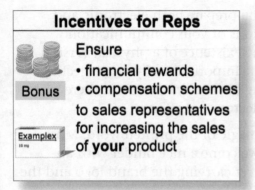

In some companies, the marketing team are not informed about the details of financial incentives (bonus or commissions) for the sales representatives. If there is a lack of transparency in your company, find out about the current compensation scheme. You need to be clear how product sales will influence the sales representatives' income.

If your product happens to be one without a substantial financial reward, the representatives will have little motivation for discussing the trial results with the prescribing physician – no matter how brilliant your marketing strategy. You'll need to discuss this crucial issue with the Marketing & Sales Manager or the business unit director. Failing to give financial incentives to the sales rep means that your aspirations for an increased rate of prescriptions are probably doomed to failure right from the start. Therefore ensure appropriate financial incentives specifically for your product.

Think global, act local

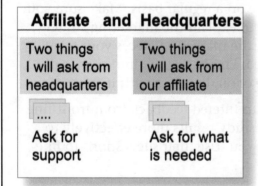

If you are working in an affiliate or operating company, ask headquarters for support.
Tell them what you need to be more successful, such as visits by opinion leaders, publications, and so on.

If you are working in head office, ask the affiliate what they need to implement the marketing strategy that you are directing. Inquire what would make them more successful in their market place. Then try to provide them with what they need. Follow up on their progress.

Get all of your stakeholders on board

Tragic but True

We are all in
the same boat ...

... but in different cabins

Internal stakeholders – although officially part of the same company – may have conflicting objectives. Organizational structures in many companies are not conducive to getting the biggest impact of clinical trials on prescribing behaviour.

There may well be a gap between Marketing and 'Medical' ('Medical' implying 'Clinical Development' or 'Clinical Research' or 'Clinical Project Management'). Those in 'Medical' may feel that they have accomplished their mission with the completion of the clinical trial and the writing of the study report.

Enlist your boss's help

Help From Your Boss

Ask for a special email

From: Joe Smith, President
To: All employees
Re: Examplex ABC trial

I expect you to maximize the impact of these trial results on revenue!

Ask your CEO to do you a favour and to support your project by sending a special email to everyone in the company. An email like this emphasizes the importance of your product and the marketing activities around your trial. Note: the sender of this email has to be the CEO himself or herself and not just the CEO's office.

In the example the president said in an earlier interview 'I expect you to make best use of these trial results to maximize revenue!' Perhaps you might ask him or her for a similar encouraging remark that you can use during your presentations. Use your organization's hierarchy to get all internal stakeholders in line and on your side.

Think 'seamless communication'

Seamless Communication

Overcome silo structures and functional stovepipes

- Talk to people across boundaries
- Include people from other units
- Think borderless interaction

You need to think 'borderless communication'. Contact your colleagues across departmental and divisional boundaries. Large companies often have separate and parallel channels of communication with no connection between them (often referred to as silo structures). Overcome these unnecessary boundaries and make your communication more effective.

Weave a web of supporters

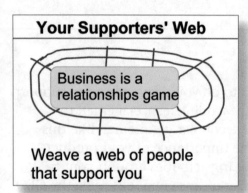

Your Supporters' Web

Business is a relationships game

Weave a web of people that support you

Work on your own web of supporters and allies. Identify the people who could support you. Contact them and try to bring them into your network.

Keep your network of personal contacts growing. Build bridges and forge alliances.

Remember, business is a relationships game.

Become a networker

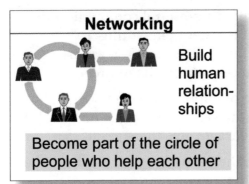

Networking

Build human relation-ships

Become part of the circle of people who help each other

You need to become an instinctive networker and connect intuitively with people. Make contact with people and become one of the circle of people who inform and help each other.

Take time to support individuals in your network and build loyalty.
Share information, make introductions, give referrals, offer references.

Devote time to networking.
Stay in touch with people on a regular basis – personally or by telephone.
Build strong human relationships and rapport.

Update your stakeholders

Regular Stakeholder Updates

Turn the wheel

| Send email and fax |
| Write a letter |
| Give presentations |
| Invite stakeholders to meetings |

Use all available channels

Distribute and disseminate information regularly via all available channels:

- give presentations
- invite stakeholders to meetings
- write emails.

Once in a while it may be a good idea to print your information on paper and send a fax or a letter instead of an email. These will attract attention because they have become rather rare in this era of electronic communication.

Keep your stakeholders in the loop. You can hardly communicate too much.

Use the telephone

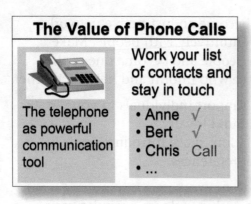

Your telephone is a powerful communication tool. Use it. It is faster than writing. It circumvents the bureaucracy. You can be informal. You can talk off the record.

Develop a list of important stakeholders. Check when you last talked to the people on your list. If it was a while ago, give them a call!

Keep up with the people on your list. Keep them posted. Stay in touch.
Revisit your list at least once every week.

Making an effective phone call can save you days of work on the project and help you overcome obstacles that might otherwise seem insurmountable.

Set up 'good news' emails

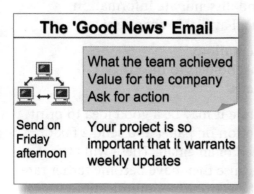

How about writing a short 'Good News' email at the end of the every working week. It should always include positive, encouraging and uplifting news. Focus on the essentials:

- what the team has achieved
- the value you are creating for the company
- ask the reader for action (Examples: 'Come to the workshop', 'Visit our company intranet site', 'Read the article').

Prepare it beforehand, but wait until late Friday afternoon to send it. You may choose to send your email as the last thing you do on Friday before shutting down your computer. Monday morning is the day on which most people have the least number of emails in their in-boxes. Your email becomes one of the few emails, with an increased chance that people will read it.

Establishing a regular email of this kind achieves two objectives. First you keep stakeholders in the loop. Second, you highlight the importance of the project and strengthen the perception that this project is so important that it warrants weekly updates.

Start your emails with the most important words

The Email Subject Line
Examplex Good News No 6
Examplex ABC trial: Conclusions
Examplex improves outcome
Start with the most important word, followed by the second most important word

Start with the most important word (usually the product name) in the 'subject matter' line of your email, followed by the second most important word. When you are searching for a particular email stored amongst thousands of others in the archive of your computer, this approach is helpful. The 'search function' in your software will quickly list the pertinent emails and help you to retrieve the email you are looking for.

In other words, a title such as 'Analysis of ABC study' is not a good one for your subject line. 'Analysis of' are not the most important words in your message. The example shows various options. Adopt the one that works best for you.

Perhaps you could discuss the rules of 'email etiquette' at your next department meeting or the planned kick-off meeting for marketing the trial results?

Coordinate internal marketing activities

Coordination of Activities	
	Become the knowledgeable guide, officially or unofficially leading the project team
Steer Harmonize Synchronize	

Who will coordinate all the individual internal marketing activities? Who will integrate everything into a successful campaign?

This is a great opportunity for you to assume organizational and intellectual leadership of the project - with or without formal lines of authority. This coordination can turn you into an expert guide, someone who knows both the inner mechanisms of the company and the external strategy to pursue in the market place. Ultimately, this job can turn you into the 'de facto project team leader'.

COMMUNICATING EXTERNALLY

Develop an external communication campaign

External Communication

Marketing Strategy for Product

	Pre-Marketing
	Publication Strategy
	Events
	Opinion Leaders
	The Web
Activities in the market	Public Relations
	Advertising
	Sales Force
	Coordination

The illustration lists key components of an effective external communication campaign. You will need to develop these elements in your game plan.

Analyze the essentials

Delivering Your Message

To the right audience:
Physicians, patients, pharmacists, opinion leaders

In the right sequence

In the right way

Before launching your marketing strategy, ask yourself the following questions:

- Am I addressing the right audience?
  For example: what influence do physicians, pharmacists, patients and other players have on the decision-making process? How do I know that I am targeting the appropriate groups?
- Am I addressing the audience in the right sequence?
  For example: am I working the 'pyramid of opinion leaders' in a logical order?
  Do I need to address the specialists before addressing the general practitioners?
- Am I addressing the audience in the right way?
  For example: how many of the physicians I want to email have internet access?

Plan pre-marketing

Pre-Marketing

Sow the seeds

Benefit from the study before the results are available

You can benefit from the study before the study results are available. Just as you may undertake pre-marketing before the launch of a product, you can 'pre-market' a clinical trial before the launch of the trial results. Create receptiveness in your target group.

Choose the most appropriate pre-marketing alternative

Three Pre-Marketing Options

Riding the wave

Acknowledge a medical need

Address a research question

Create an umbrella concept

There are basically three main ways of 'pre-marketing' a trial:

1) acknowledge an unmet medical need
2) address an important research question
3) create a general overall concept.

The following three illustrations explore these options.

Acknowledge a medical need

A Medical Need

Confirm the need for better treatment

< 140/90 mmHg		< 160/95 mmHg		
USA	Canada	Finland	Spain	Australia
27	16	20.5	20	19
England	France	Germany	Scotland	India
6	24	22.5	17.5	9
		> 65 years		

Percentage of adequately treated hypertensives

Start by pointing out the medical problem. For example you may emphasize the number of patients not adequately treated with current forms of blood pressure lowering therapy. Emphasize the need for better treatment options.

You are taking a certain risk since at this stage: you still will not know if your study will demonstrate a superior treatment option. Your aspirations should nevertheless move you in that direction. Create the perception that you have something worthwhile to communicate.

Address a research question

A Research Question

RR?

Example

What is the optimal arterial blood pressure?

The HOT (Hypertension Optimal Treatment) trial investigated this question

Examine your study very carefully: how important is the research question that it will answer? If the question underlying the trial is relevant to the scientific community or the prescribing doctor, focus on this aspect in your pre-marketing activities.

For example: The HOT (Hypertension Optimal Treatment) trial explored – among other things – the highly pertinent research question 'What is the optimal pressure for arterial blood?'

Create an umbrella concept

An Umbrella Concept

Develop a theme versatile enough to accommodate the future message independent of the exact scientific results

Example   Confidence

You need to develop a theme or general concept that is versatile enough to accommodate your future messages, independently of the exact scientific results.

For example, the theme of 'Confidence' which implies trust and assurance for those selecting your product. Once you have access to the trial results, you can use your confidence theme as a platform: 'Confidence, because Examplex effectively lowers ...'.

Develop a publication strategy

The Publication Team

Marketing

Medical Team

Key Investigator

Potential support:
Experienced Consultant
Medical Writer

Set up a team to help you devise a publication strategy. The illustration shows which key functions you may want to include in the group preparing the publication of your trial results.

Fine-tune the wording

Preparing Articles

Draft Manu-script

Section *Abstract*
Conclusions

Use positive words

Suggest
short, straightforward,
easily quotable sentences

If possible, don't wait until the principal investigator submits the final manuscript of the article for publication in a scientific journal. Work closely with the 'Medical Team' and principal investigator before the manuscript is submitted for publication. The manuscript should contain clear, concise statements with positive vocabulary that is easily quotable. An approach like this will endorse your message.

Get hold of a draft of the manuscript and read the 'Abstract' or 'Conclusions' sections. Perhaps you can suggest ways of rewording some of the most complex scientific statements. For example, you can recommend:

- changing words that have negative connotations with words that carry more positive connotations and adequately represent the results
- making sentences shorter
- making statements more straightforward
- changing the passive voice into the active voice.

Be generous wih reprints

Reprint Distribution

Reprints

Via sales reps in the doctor's office

At the company booth of an exhibition

At satellite symposia of conferences

When the Medical Department tells you that the manuscript has been accepted for publication, you have a reason to celebrate. Invite your colleagues from the 'Medical Team' to a spontaneous party in your office. They have worked hard for the last months and now is the time to show your appreciation. Contact the publisher and ask for a bulk discount if you order multiple copies of the article before they start printing. It may appear more cost-effective to make copies on your office copy machine, but by doing so you would be infringing on copyright, and high-quality reprints from a publishing house seem to carry more value than simple copies from a copying machine.

Distribute the reprints generously. Explain to the sales representatives how the article supports the credibility of their message when handed to the doctor. Ship reprints to the scientific conferences that your company attends. Booths in the exhibition area or the auditorium where your satellite symposium takes place are all good places to hand out reprints to interested parties.

Mail out your reprints

Reprint Mailing

Publication

Send out the main article to the doctors in your database

Who should send it?

Ask the Principal Investigator!

Ask the principal investigator if he or she is willing to sign a cover letter for a mailing to send the reprinted key article to your database of opinion leaders and physicians on the official stationery of the university or teaching hospital. You'll need to pay for the additional printing and the postage.

Draft the cover letter

A Draft Letter

Cover letter accompanying your reprint

Dear colleague,

University Hospital ....

The results of a randomized clinical trial in diabetic patients treated with substantin may be of interest to you.

I enclose the recent publication.

Best regards,
Professor Peter Smith

Enclosure: Reprint

Prepare a draft for the cover letter that will accompany the reprint.

Do not expect the principal investigator to do any direct advertising for you, so do not ask him or her to mention the brand name in the letter.

Branding is your job.

Emphasize key sentences

Highlights

Substantin Improved
Outcome in Patients with
Diabetes

Substantin
improved
cardiovascular out-
come by 50%

Emphasize
key sentences
in the
publication

Is the average doctor likely to read the publication he or she receives?
Probably not. You need to make it easier for the doctor to focus on your message when looking at the publication. Use a text marker to highlight vital sentences that reflect the essence of your message.

You can also print the most important statement on a separate adhesive Post-it® note that you can then attach to the original article. It will invariably draw the viewer's attention towards your message.

Stimulate follow-up articles

Suggested Topics

Themes for follow-up papers

• Additional analyses
• Intermediate endpoints
• Reports about conferences
• Reviews

Publish, Publish, Publish

Stimulate follow-up articles after publication of the main article. The example suggests various options. Writing a report about a satellite symposium that covers your trial is also a possibility. Keep in touch with key investigators, who may also offer ideas for additional articles or journals to approach.

Of course less prestigious journals can serve as an outlet for these articles. Timely publication in a secondary or tertiary journal can be more influential for marketing the trial results than the prestige of the journal itself.

Remember: publish, publish, publish.

Encourage your authors

Author Support

 Inspire to write

- Pay honoraria
- Support travel expenses
- Suggest junior researcher
- Consider medical writer

Support your authors, with honoraria or support for travel expenses. Invite the principal investigator or a colleague to write follow-up articles. The principal investigator will often assign this task to a registrar or a younger researcher in their hospital or university.

Try to contact this person directly while keeping the principal investigator in the loop. Establishing a good relationship with this junior person may prove useful. You can develop a pool of contacts from which future opinion leaders typically emerge. The honoraria you pay these junior researchers is usually well below the cost of professional medical writers, so you can afford to be generous. If these people have little time, a professional medical writer can prepare a draft of the article which the official author can then polish. Remember the author must have final ownership and sign-off.

Develop an appropriate fee structure

Fees for Authors

Agreement
Of the total sum, we will pay
1/3 on submission of initial manuscript
1/3 on submission of revised manuscript
1/3 on final acceptance of manuscript

Write a contract that connects fees to project progress achieved

The illustration shows an example of how to split up fees during the process of preparing and submitting an article for publication. An alternative is to pay 50 percent of the agreed sum on first submission of the article, and 50 percent on submission of the revised article.

Work out your own system that gives the best financial incentives to your authors to complete the article within the suggested time lines.

Transform your events

More Than Information

Educational event → Educational event and worthwhile experience

People pay more for entertainment than for education

Educational events sponsored by the pharmaceutical industry have traditionally been both educational and entertaining. Mere entertainment is not enough. The idea of turning a mundane 'scientific' workshop or congress for doctors into an encounter that engages their imagination and will have a lasting impression may seem far fetched at first.

You may simply be planning an afternoon of continuing medical education for twenty general practitioners. Nevertheless, see how far you can develop the event without appearing inappropriate or foolish.

Use your imagination

Staging an Experience

 Create a worthwhile meeting

Orchestrate a memorable encounter

Make it an event that people will remember

Observe legal constraints

Imaginative event management involves much more than just organizing the event.
You need to plan with a mindset that will create an experience that will be remembered. You are staging a workshop for your audience. Think about how the elements of scenery, drama or theatre can also transform your workshop into an inspirational and memorable experience. Ask an event agency about creative ideas.

Make sure you don't overstep the 'codes of conduct' and legal restrictions many industry associations have developed for their members. If in doubt, contact an experienced lawyer. The most knowledgeable lawyers are usually those who helped develop these 'codes of conduct' in the first place.

Get the most out of your events

The Potential of Events

Examplex — Brand the event

Make your product visible

Connect to your guests

Establish personal rapport

Benefit from your workshops and other events with your customers by taking into account the following items, depending on the size of the event:

- brand the event: Try to display your product visibly, but not too prominently
- weave your message into the fabric of the event (Ask your creative agency for their suggestions)
- connect with your guests: Your aim is to strengthen personal relationships with your customers.

Bear in mind it is you who is funding the event.

Time your invitations

The Schedule for Invitations

| 4 | to | 8 | weeks |

in advance of a regional workshop

Send a reminder three to seven days before the event

Take into account school vacations, national or religious holidays, special events

If you are planning a regional workshop for doctors, work out how far in advance of the event you would mail your invitations to maximize attendance. Based on the experience of promotional mailings for seminars in the US, the most effective lead time seems to be four to eight weeks before the event. If you plan an event on a national level, you will need a longer lead time.

It is also worthwhile sending a reminder approximately three to seven days prior to the event. Be careful to avoid conflicts with school vacations, national or religious holidays, or special events in the area of the workshop.

Print a road map

Your Invitation Road Map

Examplex Workshop Venue

Show people how to get there

Branded invitation card

Most customers appreciate the convenience of finding a map to the venue on their invitation card. This simple service will help them find the quickest way to the event. It encourages people to arrive on time and in a more relaxed frame of mind, because they have not got lost on the way.

If you regularly use the same location for your event, make sure that you have a clear map. Some hotels only offer rather poor maps. It is often worth spending money on a graphic designer to draw a good map and to brand the invitation card by using the typography, colours, symbols and so on of your brand.

Copying a segment from a published map is an infringement of copyright.

Create an event checklist

Conference Checklist

Wealth of options

- Main session
- Satellite symposium
- Expert workshop
- Press activities
- Booth at exhibition
- Hand-out materials
- Hotel reservations

In order to prepare every aspect of your conference, ask yourself the 'Where/When/Who is responsible' questions for the following items:

- main scientific session
- satellite symposium with opinion leaders as speakers
- expert workshop with investigators
- press activities, such as a press conference
- booth at the industry exhibition
- hand-out materials, such as brochures and reprints
- hotel reservations for speakers and selected physicians.

Optional items include breakfast sessions and local media coverage.

You will probably need an internal or external travel agency or congress service to take care of travel details, hotel reservations and so on. If appropriate, think refreshments, sound systems, lighting and so on. Consider a rehearsal of important sessions.

Organize satellite symposia

Satellite Symposia

- Which conference?
- What attractive topic?
- Who as speakers, chairpersons?
- Which support for travel, slides?

Meet speakers and chairpersons before the event

You want attractive and well-attended satellite symposia. Be selective in your choice of conferences. It is better to have two well-organized satellite symposia than three poorly organized ones.

Choose a theme that is currently in vogue and will attract people even if this topic is not wholly related to your product.

Choose at least one speaker who is known to draw the crowds. If you need to invite an influential person who has poor speaking skills, appoint him or her chairperson. This prominent role will be happily accepted and the audience will be grateful for being spared a less than thrilling presentation.

Offer your speakers support and production of their slides. Do not insist on a one-size-fits-all approach for all slides. Speakers will be more at ease and appear more credible, if they are not forced to show the slick and colourful slides from the company's communication agency (everyone in the audience will know that you sponsored the slides, in any event).

Make sure that you meet the speaker and chairperson prior to the meeting. You thus have a chance to discuss last-minute changes. Share with them what you are trying to achieve with the symposium. If the event is governed by CME rules – abide by them.

Get the most from your booth

The Exhibition Booth

- Make your brand visible
- Structure: The higher the better
- Keep it interactive
- Use images
- Avoid fine print
- Offer special treatment to VIPs
- Be reasonable with give-aways

Use an internal or external professional agency experienced in building booths for medical conferences.

- make your brand stand out
- the higher the structure of the booth, the more visible your stand will be
- keep it interactive: Things to do, buttons to press...
- use mostly visual information: Images will have more impact than text
- avoid fine print in text, because nobody will read it
- offer special treatment to VIPs, for example a quiet corner where you can serve coffee
- be reasonable with gifts and give-aways. If you are too generous, you will attract the wrong crowd of people.

Establish the sequence of opinion leaders

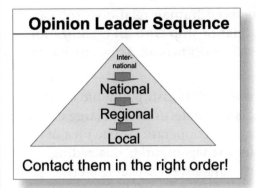

Make sure you contact the opinion leaders in the correct order starting with the international leaders moving to the national ones and then proceeding to the regional and finally to the local ones. Be aware that – especially for older products and for European countries – the endorsement from a national or regional opinion leader is sometimes more effective than from some distant expert from the other side of the Atlantic.

One company even successfully used the photo of a local physician advocating hormone replacement therapy (and implicitly also the company's product) in a national advertising campaign.

Seek endorsements

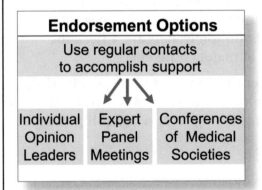

You will increase your credibility if your message is endorsed by people recognized as experts in the medical-scientific community. Their opinions will help to shape the perception of your product and your study. You can cultivate regular contacts with these experts in various ways. You can set up face-to-face conversations to discuss topics of mutual interest, for example future publications or lecture tours. You can organize expert workshops or advisory board meetings. You can organize satellite symposia at the conferences of medical societies.

Contacting a wide range of opinion leaders will give you access to expert advice, and later, credible independent external sources for your communication activities.

Connect with people

Human Relationships

It's always personal!

You **never** have a relationship with an organization

You **always** have a relationship with an individual

Connect to people

Business is all about human relations. You can never have a relationship with an organization. Relationships are with people. They are always personal.

The quality of the relationship you have with opinion leaders will determine to a large extent the success of your cooperation. The idea of 'opinion leader management' is misleading. It is not about managing opinion leaders; rather you are looking for a mutually beneficial collaboration in which trust is paramount.

Locate future thought leaders

Potential Thought Leaders

Become a scout

Ask others

Who are the up-and-coming opinion leaders?

Contact these people

Become a scout for these up-and-coming opinion leaders in your field. Find out from current opinion leaders and colleagues who the potential opinion leaders are. Check the speakers' list at major conferences.

If you can identify and meet these people while they need support and recognition, you will be able to forge a long-term relationship with them.

Set up an effective liaison

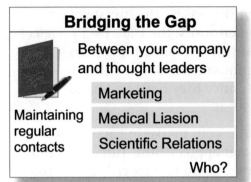

Bridging the Gap

Between your company
and thought leaders

Marketing

Maintaining
regular
contacts

Medical Liasion

Scientific Relations

Who?

In order to maximize the cooperation between opinion leaders and your company, you need someone who can maintain regular contacts with these people. Make sure everyone knows who in your company has this responsibility. In some companies there is a 'Medical Liaison' or 'Scientific Relations' department that assumes this function.

Ideally the person concerned will be an experienced, tactful and diplomatic person, able to build rapport with the eminent and famous.

The person should be imaginative enough to reconcile the wishes of each individual with the objectives of the company, and also strong enough to individualize the level of support you offer and to deny unreasonable requests.

Opinion leaders hate to be contacted by three different people from the same company with requests to lead lectures. One person should act as a 'clearing station' or 'gate keeper' and coordinate these requests, and can then contact the opinion leader so your company can speak with a single voice. If you are not that person, appoint someone. If you do not have the power to appoint someone yourself, suggest someone appropriate who should fill the role.

Use credible quotations

Quotations in Advertisements

Andy, is this now state-of-the-art
in treating patients with ABC?

Yes, Bert, indeed it is.

Medical Journal | Text of an advertising campaign in a professional journal aimed at doctors treating the disease ABC

The example illustrates a real case in which the names have been changed. Two well-known experts are in open conversation during a panel discussion at a major congress. They are discussing the conclusions of the Examplex ABC trial using Substantin. With their consent, the conversation is taped. Professor Andy A. asks Professor Bert B. 'Bert, is substantin now state-of-the-art therapy?' Bert replies 'Yes, Andy, indeed it is.'

The company used these two remarks as the text for an advertising campaign in medical journals aimed at doctors treating the disease, without mentioning the experts' names. Since the target audience knew which two opinion leaders were invoked, the campaign received attention and communicated the message in both a creative and credible way.

Appreciate the forgotten heroes

The Forgotten Heros

Benefit from the contacts already established by the 'Medical Team'

| Clinical Investigators | • Include them
• Involve them
• Invite them |

Turn investigators into advocates

The 'forgotten heroes' are the investigators who actually performed the trial. Don't neglect them. They are far less demanding than traditional opinion leaders. They already know your product, since they have had hands-on experience with it.

Include them in your marketing activities. Show them your appreciation. Turn them into advocates, invite them to a special 'thank you meeting'. Do not argue with the 'Medical' Department who will pay for the event. You should pay for it. The money for organizing this event will be well invested.

Set up VIP micro meetings

VIP Micro Meetings

The principle investigator invites hand-picked, selected experts

| Strictly confidential workshop | You facilitate and organize, creating an aura of exclusivity |

An effective way of involving opinion leaders is an invitation only experts meeting. This is a small and intimate workshop with an aura of exclusivity where the most knowledgeable and influential persons (VIPs) are invited. It is a privilege to participate. The timing for this meeting is crucial. Organize it before the first official presentation but after the article has been accepted, in order not to jeopardize the publication.

You'll need to facilitate, organize and sponsor, or in other words, direct the event. Be highly selective in your choice of company people attending the micro meeting. It may seem difficult to refuse invitations to certain managers in your organization, but you should stick to your plans.

You can talk to the experts in a controlled environment - no competitors and no distractions. Listen to them before and after the event, during coffee breaks and meals. The information you receive is often extremely valuable.

Make the most of VIP micro meetings

Meeting Benefits
Speakers practise answers to difficult questions
Invited experts enhance their reputation
You get participants on board
You reduce the risk of 'snipers'

You can benefit from VIP micro meetings in four ways:

1) The invited selected experts feel appreciated, which strengthens their relationship with your company.
2) Speakers are given an opportunity to practise their presentations in a safe environment before the official presentation at a major congress. Some of the experts who attend will ask questions that the speaker may not be able to answer. He or she then still has time to review the literature or to do more statistical analyses to find the answer. This approach enables them to respond confidently and competently to critical questions during the subsequent official congress.
3) Since participants know the details beforehand, they are more likely to trust you.
4) You can neutralize 'snipers' who shoot off hostile questions simply to feel important. If these people have already asked their question then they are less likely to repeat it during the official congress. This technique for managing hostile experts helps to ensure smoother running for the important open scientific discussion following the official presentation.

Establish an expert panel

The Expert Panel
Based on your experiences with the VIP micro meeting:
Expert Round Table
Expert Workshop
Expert Meeting

The VIP micro meetings enable you to become acquainted with various experts in an informal setting. Based on your experience with a safe 'pilot event' you should now know which experts you would like to work with (and which ones you want to avoid).

You can organize an official event. You may call it 'expert roundtable', 'expert workshop', 'expert meeting' or 'expert panel'. The term 'expert' is preferable to 'opinion leader' in this context. Use the term that is currently accepted in your company.

Organize lecture tours

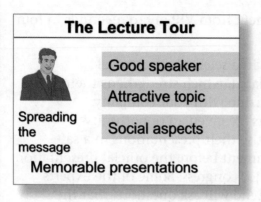

A lecture tour takes an opinion leader to groups of physicians in various cities. It can help to spread the message far and wide. When organizing a lecture tour, keep in mind the following items:

- put together a programme with a speaker who has excellent communication skills and who knows how to convey your message
- weave the message into a topic which appears attractive to your audience
- stage an agreeable event that participants will remember.

If you can't achieve all three of these objectives, consider abandoning the idea of a lecture tour.

Use the web

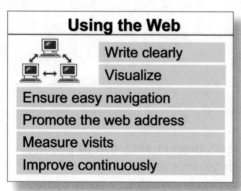

Millions of people look for healthcare advice on the internet. 'Health' has overtaken 'sex' as the No 1 key word in some search engines. Have a look at some of the websites that offer information on diseases and treatment. Visit for example 'www.lifeline.com' or 'www.netdoktor. com'. The Web is the great equalizer. You can create brilliant websites with a limited budget, whereas you may not be able compete with the big global players in terms of traditional advertisements, events, or sales representatives.

A good web site requires time, commitment and support from a specialized web agency. For a successful, user-friendly website you'll need to:

- write clear and crisp text
- make information visual. Convey a large portion of the information in images, not simply words
- ensure easy navigation
- promote your web address. Make sure to include it in all your documents. Every piece you produce should direct prospects to your web presence
- measure the response to your website, for example by counting the number of visits per page
- continually improve your website using the results of visits per page and other parameters, such as dwell time.

Consider a webcast

On-Line Webcast

Dear Doctor,
Please visit our live webcast of the main session of the European Society of Hypertension. Prof. X will present the trial results ...

10000 flyers announcing the event ...

unfortunately without web address

You might contemplate a live 'webcast' for an important satellite symposium. Announce the event on your marketing flyers. Avoid the mistake that one company made: they forgot to mention the web address for the event. On the other hand, you need to be aware that most physicians will not spend their precious time watching company-sponsored symposia over the internet. Therefore you may wish to spend your money on other marketing activities - even if your web agency tries to encourage you down that route.

Learn the statutory limitations for new media

Legal Restrictions

In most European countries promotion for prescription drugs are

Legal when addressed to healthcare professionals

Illegal when addressed to the general public

When you are considering the web as a promotional tool, be aware of the legal restrictions that exist in many countries, especially in Europe. Thus advertisements for prescription drugs in many European countries are legal only when addressed to healthcare professionals and illegal when addressed to the general public. If in doubt, check with your legal department.

Identify the most appropriate web option

Options for Web Presence
General information about the disease for the public
'Professional' site with restricted access
Study group site communicating research results
Website for people in the US

You may wish to choose and combine one or more of the following components for your web strategy:

- a website with general medical information for the general public
- a professional website directed toward healthcare professionals
- a study group website for which a research group is responsible
- a website adhering to the more consumer-oriented US laws for the general public living in the United States.

Set up a patient information website

General Patient Information
Post practical information about the disease without mentioning brand names   Example:
Schering AG's educational site on multiple sclerosis for patients, families, friends at www.ms-gateway.com

You may choose to create a web site that offers general information and educates the general public about diagnosis and treatment of the disease without mentioning your product. One example is 'www.ms-gateway.com' by Schering AG where patients, families and friends can find practical information about multiple sclerosis.

Create a website for healthcare professionals

The Site for Professionals

The section you selected contains information intended for healthcare professionals only

Yes, I am a healthcare professional

Pour des raisons juridiques, les informations que vous avez sélectionnées sont réservées aux professionnels de la santé. Je confirme que j'ai lu les conditions et que je les accepte.

You may create a website with access restricted to healthcare professionals. There are some websites, where it is sufficient to click on the button 'Yes, I am a healthcare professional' to gain access to the site. In some countries, web agencies offer a verifying procedure for a healthcare professional's credentials to ensure that only these individuals have access. Talk to your internet agency to identify how you can make access easy and still observe legal restrictions. Some websites are operating in a legally grey area and you need to be aware of the risk.

Support a study group's web presence

A Study Group's Website

Study groups can operate independent websites where they communicate research results (slides from congresses, etc.)

- Suggest a draft
- Sponsor the web agency
- The study group approves content

A study group or team of investigators are allowed to communicate their scientific data via the web. You can help support their research activities and facilitate a quick and convenient scientific exchange. Suggest a draft of how to present the trial results online. Your internet agency can put the draft on a test server. The responsible person in the study group can then modify and approve the content. This independent study group website benefits both research and marketing. It can increase the study group's reputation and it can facilitate your work. When interested people contact you, you can direct them to the website instead of having to prepare individual emails with large attachments.

Consider a website for the US market

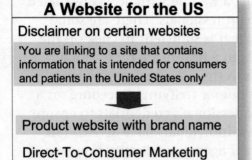

A Website for the US

Disclaimer on certain websites

'You are linking to a site that contains information that is intended for consumers and patients in the United States only'

Product website with brand name

Direct-To-Consumer Marketing

Many companies have an affiliate or their headquarters located in the US. These US-based organizations will create their own web presence according to US regulations. US legislation allows much more direct-to-consumer marketing for prescription drugs on company websites than European legislation.

Since the world wide web is global, anyone can access these pages, including citizens living in European countries with their own national regulations. The language of these websites is often English and Spanish. People that understand these languages can get qualified information on treatment options regardless of where they live. Check the extent to which you are legally entitled to promote web addresses directed to US residents also in your home market.

The site 'www.purplepill.com' highlights recent medical studies that prove that the 'purple pill' heals damage in acid reflux disease better than the other leading prescription medicines. Any consumer in the global internet community has access to this material – independent of varying national regulations.

Select the appropriate web page format

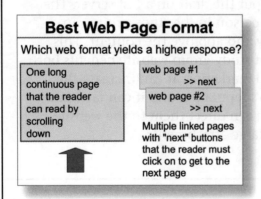

Best Web Page Format

Which web format yields a higher response?

One long continuous page that the reader can read by scrolling down

web page #1
>> next

web page #2
>> next

Multiple linked pages with "next" buttons that the reader must click on to get to the next page

Different web page formats yield differing levels of response. One continuous page that the visitor can read by scrolling down usually yields a higher response rate than two or three linked pages with "next" buttons that the reader must click on in order to be able to read the following page.

Make sure that your web agency has the necessary expertise in your market. Before engaging them to create your website, have a look at the websites they have created for other pharmaceutical companies.

Choose your type of public relations activities

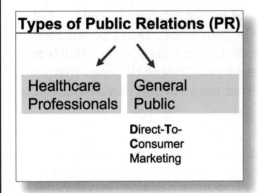

Public relations directed toward healthcare professionals allows you to work with specialized medical journalists who usually know the rules of the game.

However, public relations directed toward the general public involves working with journalists who have their own agenda. In order to avoid communication disasters, you will need professional public relations people - either in-house or external - to support you.

Evaluate your public relations plans before you start

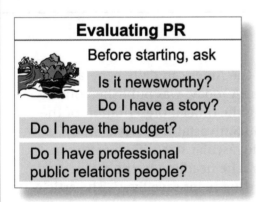

The industry is increasingly confronted by an inquisitive and often hostile media relentless in their search for the next big drug story. If you are considering utilizing this arena, there are a number of elements you will need for successful public relations activities directed toward the general public:

- Are your results genuinely interesting and newsworthy? And if so, to whom?
- Do you have a story? Many journalists are uninterested in scientific data or research results, they want a good story with a dazzling headline
- Do you have the budget? Ascertain the costs of a PR campaign before you start. Achieving a high profile in any media is expensive
- Do you have professional public relations people on board who know how to handle the press?

If you cannot meet all the above criteria, consider spending your money on other elements of the marketing mix.

Manage the journalists

Dealing with Journalists

Get public relations professionals

To select the right journalists

To take care of the journalists

To monitor the press

Use professional public relations people to help you manage the journalists. Don't be tempted to go it alone. Selecting the right journalists to approach is essential. Choose the ones that are likely to report about your story in a balanced way.

Take care of the journalists you are working with. The public relations professional you hire must give them personal attention. If you are organizing a press conference, be sure that somebody escorts the journalists to the press conference room to prevent them from going astray.

Monitor the press after the event. Did the invited journalists write about the study results and your product? Did the press conference have an impact in the media? If certain journalists repeatedly did not write any articles, drop them from your list.

Plan your direct-to-consumer marketing

A National Press Article

 USA TODAY No. 1 in the USA

Headline the day after the presentation of the "4S" study results with simvastatin

Cholesterol drug helps save lives

"The drug, Zocor, made by Merck & Co. was shown to ... "

Zocor® is a trademark from Merck & Co.

An article in the American daily general newspaper 'USA today' was published on the day following the official presentation of the 'Scandinavian Simvastatin Survival Study' at a big cardiovascular scientific meeting in Dallas, Texas. The headline to the article read 'Cholesterol drug helps save lives'. The article mentioned the indication (high cholesterol), the product benefit (helps save lives), the brand name (Zocor®) and the company (Merck & Co.). This article reflects the growing trend toward Direct-To-Consumer marketing.

A National Magazine Article

Which Love Pill is the Best One?

 tv Hear and See

In a head-to-head comparison, the percentage of men prefering
• Cialis® was 46%
• Levitra® was 30%
• Viagra® was 14%

Trademarks:
Cialis® from Lilly,
Levitra® from Bayer
Viagra® from Pfizer

Based on a translation from an article in
TV Hören und Sehen, 20 - 26 December 2003

Even I was surprised to see the headline 'Which Love Pill is the Best One?' in a magazine that usually informs consumers about the upcoming radio and television programmes. The magazine reported the results of a study involving different prescription products for the treatment of erectile dysfunction. Check with your legal department about the legal issues before you consider pursuing or permitting similar approaches.

Plan your direct-to-consumer marketing (cont)

Make the Most of Your CEO

Roche CEO Franz Humer (58) is in love to a beautiful woman and takes own slimming pill Xenical®. He is like his company: Slim and successful.

Summarized from a translated article published in "Blick", a daily Swiss newspaper for the general public on 22 July 2004

Xenical® is a trademark from Roche

The following headline in the Swiss daily newspaper "Blick" dated 22 July 2004 certainly got the readers' attention: 'Roche-CEO is in love to a beautiful woman and takes own slimming pill Xenical' (translated from German). Imagine what statements the president of your company might make to support your product. Admittedly this is easier when you market a product with a strong life style component like Xenical®. Again be aware of the legal issues.

Steer your public relations to professionals

PR to Professionals

Press release to news agencies (e.g. Reuters)

Press conference the day before the presentation (embargoed)

Press kit including background information

When you plan public relations activities directed at physicians or other healthcare professionals, you may consider one or more of the following items:

- Press releases: These texts follow their own rules, so get someone who knows how to write them. If you decide to send the press release to the large news agencies (e.g. Reuters) be aware that the chance that they will pick it up is extremely low
- Press conferences: The principal investigator should briefly present the main study results. A prestigious opinion leader can then comment and put the results into perspective. Brief these people before the conference. If they are not used to speaking to the press, consider offering them half a day of coaching. Organize the press conference on the day before the first official presentation of your study results and embargo the results. This implies that they are not to be used in public until the following day which is the day of the presentation
- Press kits: The press kit should include a combination of press release, background information on disease, treatment and study results (also called a 'backgrounder'), details on speakers as well as other relevant material.

Insist on effective advertising

Effective Advertising
Straightforward
Crystall clear
Well-branded
Tested

Objective: **Not** to win awards,
but generate sales

Some advertising agencies put their emphasis on beautiful design and graphics. Some agencies suggest noble but vague terminology. These approaches may win advertising awards, but do not necessarily generate sales. Sometimes a straightforward, clear and well-branded campaign is more effective than highly creative art work. Test different styles of adverts to establish which one has more impact.

Evaluate proposed advertisements

Testing Advertisements
Ask reps and doctors: Do they remember
The brand?
The message?
The product advantage?
Do you have 3 times 'yes'?

Always ask your agency to produce at least two draft versions so that you may test and compare them. Show the draft to several members of your target groups and then ask them:

- what's the name of the product?
- what's the message?
  what's the story?
- what's the product competitive advantage? why should they choose your product over your competitors?

You may be unpleasantly surprised at some of the answers and may want to improve the drafts. Ensure that you have the time and money to initiate market research – it is a worthwhile investment.

Make best use of the sales force

One Rep Visit to the Doctor		
	Germany	USA
Duration	6 min	1½ min
	Cost: 70 to 150 Euros	

A single visit by a medical representative to a doctor lasts approximately only six minutes in Germany and the cost of this visit is estimated to be around 70 to 150 Euros. Only two or three of these six minutes are actually spent discussing products. In the US, 43 percent of rep visits end at the receptionist's desk. An average rep visit in the US lasts around one and a half minutes. In the UK, the promotional efforts of the pharmaceutical industry represent about 11 minutes of a general practitioner's weekly time.

Develop a concise message for sales representatives

What the Rep Should Say	
	Be brief Be bright Be gone
Explaining the product benefit to the doctor	Your advantage: Why should the doctor prescribe **your** product?

Remember some facts about your sales force:

- the sales force is very expensive
- the rep has a very little time to influence prescription behaviour
- the doctor's attention span is very short
- you cannot control what the rep actually says in the doctor's office.

This means that your message must be short and concise.

Your brochures and folders must convey your message convincingly.

Be very clear about what the rep should say during the visit.

It also suggests you need to work on continuous training for your representatives.

Interact intensely with your sales force

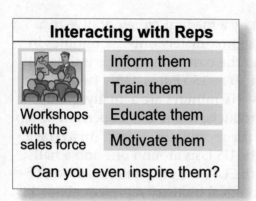

Manage the interface between you and the sales force. Spend time with your sales representatives. Make the sales representatives an integral part of your enlarged project team.

Involve them. Train them. Teach them.

You need to realize: your message is always new to someone.

Motivate them. Inspire them.

Get feedback from the market

You need to make sure that your message gets through to the doctors. Do your own personal market research to find out if that is the case. Get feedback from the front-line people. Ask them for candid answers to questions like:

- what was the doctor interested in?
- what did he or she ask about the study?
- what surprised him or her?

Their contributions can give you unfiltered information from the market – at no cost – and will help you upgrade your marketing activities.

Establish the right sequence

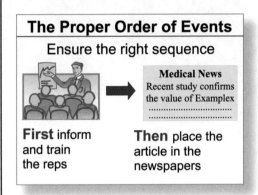

The Proper Order of Events

Ensure the right sequence

Medical News
Recent study confirms
the value of Examplex

First inform and train the reps

Then place the article in the newspapers

Consider the following: your public relations activities result in a positive article in the medical press that appears very quickly. Unfortunately, the sales representatives were not informed. The day after the publication of the article, a rep from your company enters the doctor's office and is greeted by the doctor who has read the article the day before and now asks the rep to tell more about it.

How will the rep feel about the meeting and how will he or she feel about you?

Make sure you inform and train your sales representatives before your articles are published in the media.

MAXIMIZING YOUR IMPACT

You work on projects that are worthwhile, projects that count, projects that make a difference. In order to achieve this, you need to make all elements of the marketing mix fit together. This task requires more than pushing buttons in the hope that sooner or later, something will work. Use the ideas in this section to connect the components of your marketing in a way that reinforces and enhances all of them.

Create a control room

Communication Headquarters

Put a sign on your door

Examplex Trial

Communication
Coordination
Centre

Transform your office

What about putting a sign on your office door that reads something like 'ABC Trial Communication Center'? Think of the marketing campaign as if you are the NASA Houston Control Center guiding the Apollo missions in space. If there is an unused room in your building you can scrounge, occupy it and create a place where your team can meet discretley to discuss ideas over coffee.

Your office is the place where you coordinate and harmonize your marketing activities such as training of the sales force, sales aids, the media, support to opinion leaders, advertisements, mailings. The power is in the right mix.

Be persistent

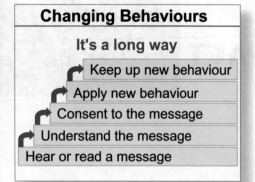

The illustration depicts the distance from transmitting information (the sales rep explaining a product to the physician) to the decision to adopt a new behaviour (the physician writing the first prescription) and finally to sustaining this new behaviour (the physician continues to write prescriptions for the product).

The process can go wrong at each step. It is vital that your message remain consistent at each stage of the process. It is a building process, each step reinforcing the previous one.

Stick to your guns

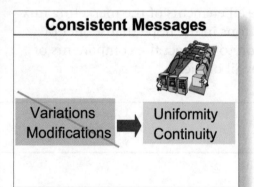

Do not allow modifications to or variations from your message. Stick to your key message and the channels you have developed and tested for communicating it. Beware other people who want to change it to their own liking. Your goal is to align everyone's communication activities through constant training, so that all are pulling in the same direction.

Consistency in Words

Use identical vocabulary and terminology in

- Publications
- Press releases
- Advertisements

Ask for drafts of articles for publication, press releases, advertisements and other material to be sent to you for your comments. Pay attention to the words used in these documents and, if necessary, suggest revisions. You are trying to ensure a consistent or at least similar vocabulary in all of these materials.

Stick to your guns (cont)

Consistency in Numbers

Use identical numbers: Either

always	or	always
49.5%		50%

Make your choice and stick to it!

Make sure that all the documents use identical numbers, in other words, it should always be '49.5 per cent' or '50 per cent'.

For the superficial reader, these are two different values.

Make a decision on which to use and stick to it religiously in all written and oral communication.

Consistency Across People

Marketing ⇔ Development

Headquarters ⇔ Affiliates

Company ⇔ Opinion leader

Requires your
constant coordination

You need to reach a high degree of consistency and uniformity in your key message regardless of who communicates it. The more consistently your message is communicated, the higher the impact. The ideal 100 percent consistency is, of course, unrealistic, since you are dealing with stakeholders who have greatly varying interests.

For example the marketing department or the 'medical team', headquarters or affiliates, the company or opinion leaders have differing objectives. Trying to achieve a high degree of consistency across all these parties requires your constant attention and coordination. Keep in mind that you cannot communicate too often.

Consistency Across Time

Repeat
identical key
messages over
a longer period

Hammer it in!

Year on year

Ensure continuity over time.
Convey the same core message year on year.
Repeat the identical key message over a long period – even to the point of getting sick of hearing your own message.
Only then will your message stick.

Resist the sales representatives' call for change

Resisting Temptation

The sales rep is longing for change

The doctors want something new.
We need a fresh cycle campaign.

I am bored and
I want something new!

You will face pressures for change from the sales force. In fact, many sales representatives will long for change. When they tell you that doctors want something new, it usually means that they (the sales representatives) want something new. The doctor may only be starting to remember your message and considering writing the first prescription; in which case any change in message may cause the process to break down.

Use the best mix of channels

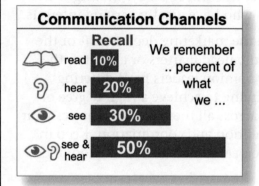

Communication Channels

Recall

read 10%
hear 20%
see 30%
see & hear 50%

We remember .. percent of what we ...

Leaving printed material in the doctor's office has limited impact. Even if the doctor looks at it, he or she is unlikely to remember the content. Reading information in print is the least effective means of communicating. You need to show and tell. Illustrate your message with visuals from your sales aid. Presenting the message and explaining the diagrams in person is five times as effective as the doctor reading it silently in his or her office.

Remember the power of personal presentation

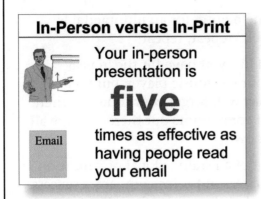

You want to get noticed in your company? Remember: presenting your message in person is five times as effective as having someone read your email.

Encourage a dialogue

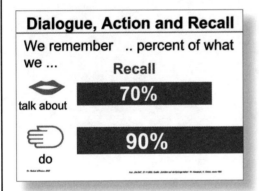

Encourage the doctor to talk about your product. Ask questions. The more the doctor talks about your product, the greater the likelihood that he or she will remember it.

Learning psychology underlines the effect of actions on memory. The first prescription is always the hardest to achieve, but once doctors have written one prescription, they are likely to continue prescribing the product because they will remember it.

Repeat, repeat, repeat

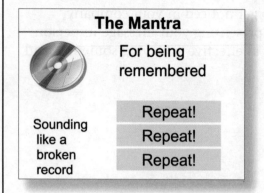

Remember the mantra for an unforgettable message: repeat, repeat, repeat!

You may feel like you have hit the 'repeat' button on your CD music player, but your customers may well forget your tune and there are dozens of competitors out there who are all playing their own.

The president of a leading global organization was asked the reason for his company's success. He answered that there were three key factors for their success: 'Tell the doctor, tell the doctor, tell the doctor.'

Retell, restate and reaffirm your message to the prescribing physician repeatedly.

MOBILIZING EXTERNAL SUPPORT

Benefit from the skills and expertise of knowledgeable outsiders. These can be advertising agencies, graphic design studios, communication firms or consultants. Use the ideas in this section to help you find the right agency and get the very best from them.

Find the right agency

The Right Agency
Check the web
Ask people from the agency scene
Ask colleagues and managers
Consult your external network
Ask agencies for references
Check the references
Invite selected agencies to a pitch

The example gives you some tips for identifying the appropriate agency or consultant.

Always seek personal recommendations. Beware of agencies with too few clients as well as those with too many. Keep in mind that you are basically buying the expertise of one or two individuals. Inquire about their hands-on experience with similar projects. The high prestige of any agency is of no value to you on its own.

Make sure that the agency is strong both in the creative and project management aspects. Some agencies bubble over with creative ideas, but cannot deliver on time, to specification or within budget. Others manage the nuts and bolts, but lack imagination and original ideas. You need to establish whether your agency has good track records on both the creative and the practical aspects. Ask for specific examples.

Prepare your people for the pitch

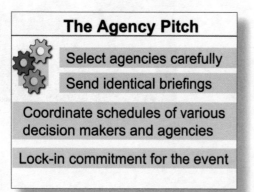

The Agency Pitch

Select agencies carefully

Send identical briefings

Coordinate schedules of various decision makers and agencies

Lock-in commitment for the event

To find the appropriate agency, select several competing agencies, brief them and invite them to present a sales pitch. During their presentations, all agencies will claim to be the very best. They will claim to have special expertise in the field. They will promise that their top people will work on the project and will be responsive to your comments.

Remember that the agency's presentation should be only a small part of your decision-making process. I have known cases where a presenter from the agency gave an excellent presentation, but never showed up again during the subsequent project.

When you plan the pitch, lock in a commitment from all stakeholders to attend. Out-of-town people should arrive the evening prior to the event to avoid the painful fiasco of one brand team leader who missed the pitch she had organized due to cancelled flights. Top people from management and from four agencies showed up. She was the only person missing – not a good career move.

Identify an expert guide

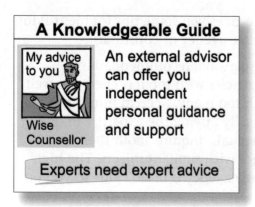

A Knowledgeable Guide

My advice to you

Wise Counsellor

An external advisor can offer you independent personal guidance and support

Experts need expert advice

Find an external mentor who can give you independent advice on how to manage the project (and also your career). He or she can add a new dimension and suggest creative ideas that neither you nor your agency may have thought of. An experienced outside consultant or a retired colleague or boss can assume this role – and help you to focus on your professional well-being, too.

Some advertising agencies have only one solution to fit all your problems: More advertising. In many cases this is neither appropriate nor financially feasible. An independent expert can add a fresh perspective and help you find the activities that promise a better return on your time and money spent.

Remember: even experts need expert advice.

Get the most from your agency

Working with the Agency

START Divide into subprojects

Update your briefing

Ask for drafts

Locate the creative people and get them into your team right from the start

Once you decide which agency you want to work with, sign a contract that allows you to terminate the agreement easily. Split the project into several smaller subprojects and pay them on the basis of each completed subproject. You can then commission the subsequent subproject once you are happy with the previous one.

Update your briefing. State again what messages to convey (brand promise), how to express them, the branding guidelines to observe, and so on. Do not assume anything. Ask the agency to explain their understanding of what you have told them ('re-briefing'). Listen carefully. You may be surprised. Continue your discussion until you feel that they have a precise understanding of what you want.

Stay in contact with the agency and ask for concepts and preliminary versions of the campaign to see if the agency is on the right path.

Identify the creative people who actually do the work (some agencies hide them) and invite them to a few team meetings, right from the start of the project.

Make your objectives clear

Clarifying the Objectives

Do excellent advertising for an excellent product

You are **not** in fine art, but here to help me generate sales

Make your objectives very clear. Their job is to do excellent advertising for an excellent product. However, they will add value only if they help you generate sales. Their work needs to increase the revenue of your product.

If the agency can do it with tasteful graphics, elaborate design or award-winning creative art work, that's fine. If a simple, straightforward, no-nonsense approach is more likely to increase revenue for your product, then use the latter.

Beware the 'full service offer'

The Full Service Illusion

I will pay the advertising agency to do good marketing and I've got nothing to worry about

Marketer's Dream

Some agencies will tell you that they can handle the entire project for you. They assign an account manager to act as liaison between you and the various units of the agency. Rather than coordinating the efforts of a writer, artist, photographer, and other specialists yourself, the account manager will do it all for you. The first drawback of this approach is budgetary. You are paying someone else just to manage the project. The second is that lines of communication quickly become complex. Your instructions to the account manager are sometimes miscommunicated to the specialists within the agency.

A second option is to work directly with freelance professionals who handle specific sub-projects for you. Some very creative people do not fit in well at larger agencies. When you work with these independent agents, you gain control and save money, but you will spend more time managing the project yourself.

No matter which option you choose, be aware that you cannot buy good marketing. You can buy individual services or advice, but ultimately you have to assemble the overall marketing puzzle yourself. That is a process you cannot outsource.

DEVELOPING THE PROJECT STRATEGY

The marketing of clinical trial results is a major endeavour. A project with a beginning and an end, with objectives and stakeholders. Use the ideas in this section to help you steer the project successfully through the various phases of its life.

Manage the project phases

The Five Project Phases	
1 Start	Assignment
2 Shape	Reframing phase
3 Plan	Submarine phase
4 Implement	Flagship phase
5 Close	Finishing phase

You need to manage the five project phases carefully:

- start: you receive an assignment from your boss
- shape: you reframe the assignment so that it suits both market and your needs
- plan: you and the core team lay the groundwork in the 'submarine' phase
- implement: your organization rolls out the project in the marketplace
- close: you finish the project successfully and move on.

Define your own project parameters

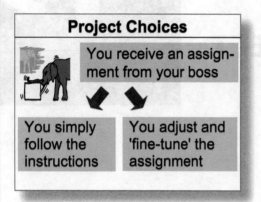

Every assignment has a starting point, an opportunity that offers several options. Unfortunately, many people do not realize that they do have a choice.

You receive an assignment from your boss.

You can choose the option of following instructions exactly as they have been given and 'do as you are told, no questions asked'. Or you can dare to modify the original assignment. Most of the time, you do have a choice. Make it.

Remember what the German poet Goethe said about starting: 'Whatever you can do or dream, begin it. Boldness has genius, power and magic in it.'

Modify the project to suit the needs

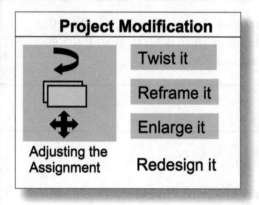

Modify the project to meet both the needs of the market as well as your own needs. Obviously you cannot redraw the map. But you can adjust the original assignment to meet market needs as you perceive them. You can fine-tune the assignment and put a different spin on the project so you learn new things.

Reshape the project, so it contains a personal development dimension where you can justifiably test out fresh ideas. Consider how you might change the scope of your initial project so that it will broaden your spectrum of skills. Shape the project to enable you to work in a way that is rewarding both to the company and to you.

Sometimes you can convert what looks initially like a mundane assignment into a fascinating project and great opportunity to grow.

Think about your personal image

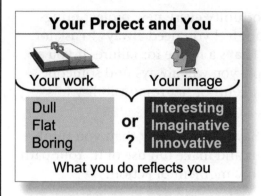

Your Project and You

Your work   Your image

Dull	**or**	Interesting
Flat		Imaginative
Boring	**?**	Innovative

What you do reflects you

Your projects reflect your professional identity. The kind of work you do labels you in the eyes of the people with whom you work.

If your projects appear dull, flat and boring, people will tend to associate these attributes with you as well. If your projects appear interesting, imaginative and innovative, this is how you will be seen.

What do you want as your image?

Shape your project profile

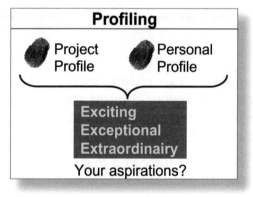

Profiling

Project   Personal
Profile   Profile

Exciting
Exceptional
Extraordinary

Your aspirations?

See to what extent your project can help fund your dreams and aspirations.

You have a strong influence on your own work environment.

Have the courage to exert that influence!

Ask yourself how you can shape the project profile so that it becomes exciting, even exceptional or extraordinary. How can you transform the project into something worth bearing your signature and demonstrative of your professional performance?

Take the initiative

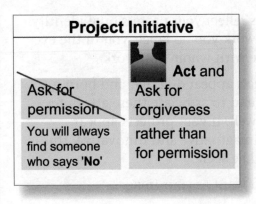

Use the opportunity every new project brings with it. Do not feel you need always to ask for permission. That's a recipe for failure. If you ask enough people you will always find someone who thinks it is his or her responsibility to say 'No.'

You usually have more leeway than you think. Be courageous and make full use of it. Your path is created in the moment of action.

When I started doing this, I was afraid of the question 'Who authorized you?' Nobody ever asked me that question.

Stretch your comfort zones

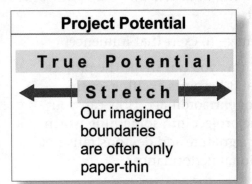

Many of our limitations are self-imposed. Think outside the box. Stretch your comfort zones. You do have some freedom of choice. Unfold the possibilities. Exploit the space. It's usually there.

Accept assignments that force you to stretch yourself.

Assume new responsibilities and take calculated risks.

Take charge!

Try new things

Trying Things

Getting up

Get used to being uncomfortable

Barbra Streisand

Get comfortable being uncomfortable

Tom Peters
Re-imagine! Business Excellence in a Disruptive Age

If you stay at the same cosy place for long, it might feel comfortable for everyone.
You will however stagnate.

Put yourself at ease doing exciting new things you have never done before.
Take the initiative.

Find out if you should change the direction of your current journey with the project.
Be willing to choose situations that challenge you.

Plan the submarine phase

The Submarine Phase

Remaining below the surface

Quiet

Discreet

Secretive

Only the core team has access to concepts and drafts

In the early stages of a project, your team's conceptual activities are pretty much invisible. Remain discreet and do not distribute detailed minutes to people outside your core team.

Before you go public, only the core team has access to the wealth of raw results and the various drafts you discuss and test. You need time to figure out the communication concept, story, script and planned activities without interference.

Keep your bosses informed but only of major developments.

Identify the crew

The Submarine Crew

Marketing	Optional:
Marketing Research	Project Coordinator
Advertising	External Consultant
Medical Team	

The team on board during the submarine phase of the project usually includes people from the following functions:

- marketing (one or two persons)
- market research
- internal marketing services, advertising department or communication agency
- medical team or clinical development team
- optional: project coordinator or project management person
- optional: consultant.

The total number of people in this core team will be between four to seven.

Manage confidentiality

Clandestine Operations

Classified Information

Organize confidential brainstorming

Figure out the concept

Develop the story

Maintain confidentiality

Early Caution

Protect your drafts during the confidential stage

It is easy to crush a seedling

Do not release draft versions

Make use of confidential brainstorming sessions where creative ideas for developing the story or script can flourish. Preliminary versions and concepts are just that, and only the core team members should have access to them. Add a strong dose of curiosity. Unleash a team debate by asking questions such as 'what if' and 'why not'. At this stage, accept controversy, fluidity and fuzziness. Be sure to explain personally to everyone in your core team that absolute confidentiality is essential.

Beware other people in the organization who show too much interest in your work. Be tight-lipped and resist the temptation to release raw concepts and draft versions. Bite your tongue instead of satisfying their curiosity.

It is easy for someone in the company to stamp on your seedling at this early stage of its growth. You do not yet know what your message will be and which words and images you will choose to convey that message.

Protect your budding project well.

Prevent leaks of information

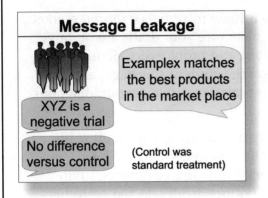

A partly formed idea or marketing concept that leaks out may well undermine your whole project. Imagine the following situation. Your trial results showed no statistically significant difference between Examplex and the active control which was standard treatment.

The message that leaked out was 'The XYZ study is a negative trial' when you would have preferred to communicate 'Examplex matches the best products in the market place.' Obviously, these two messages create very different perceptions. Do everything to prevent the leakage of draft messages.

Keep the process going foward

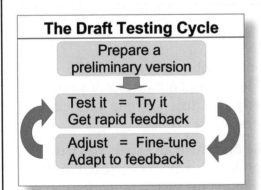

Prepare a preliminary version of your marketing concept. During your confidential brainstorming sessions you can discuss unconventional options and play with various drafts. In this protected space, you can encourage and tolerate a transient phase of creative chaos. You can improvise.

Once you have a draft, work on improving it through a quick process of testing, receiving feedback and adjusting the draft. Restart the cycle until you get it right. Learn by trial and error, continually improving the current version. Get comfortable with this iterative process of creating, destroying and re-creating.

Test your drafts

Draft Testing

Message
Words
Style
Layout
Diagrams
Images

} Do formal
or informal
market
research on
all aspects

Your draft

You need to initiate informal or formal market research to make sure your drafts are on target. You should test and probe every element of your package: the content (message) and the expression (vocabulary, style, layout, diagrams, images).

The only way to find out if your draft really works with the customers is to ask for frank feedback from your customers. Invite constructive critique from selected customers and build their recommendations into your draft. Understand that achieving your objective of changing habits takes time. Therefore market research will not always give you the answers you expect.

Seek confidential feedback

Targets for Testing

Discuss the draft with an **expert** you trust

Chat about the draft with a **doctor** you are familiar with

Talk about the draft with a **sales rep** you know well

During the pre-launch phase you can use a number of 'quick and dirty' tests of your draft. Discreetly ask trusted people for their confidential feedback:

- discuss the draft with an expert you trust
- ask several doctors who participated in the trial programme for their comments
- send the draft to several sales representatives you know well.

Their critical evaluations will help you to revise and upgrade your draft versions.

Be a silent witness to focus groups

Focus Groups

Experienced interviewer

What do your customers really think about your draft?

Hidden insights

Often there is no need for commissioning expensive detailed market research studies. However you may consider one or two focus groups. The composition of doctors in your groups should reflect your target groups. Ask your market research department or an agency to prepare and set up these events. You need an experienced interviewer to detect what doctors really think as they are unlikely to admit all their thoughts and wishes openly. They may also be tempted to tell you what they think you want to hear. You can take part in these groups as a silent witness.

My own experience was enlightening: the focus group tore some of the favourite elements of my communication concept to pieces. I was grateful because the group helped reveal latent competitive advantages and gave me specific suggestions on how to improve my drafts.

Beware the three reasons for not testing

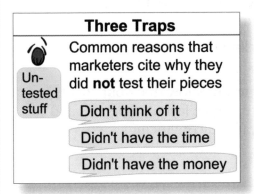

Three Traps

Common reasons that marketers cite why they did **not** test their pieces

Un-tested stuff

Didn't think of it

Didn't have the time

Didn't have the money

Do not use untested material. You will not know if you are on target. Testing is a routine procedure in the fast moving consumer goods industry. They take the time to ask and take the time to listen. Make it your routine, too. During my consultancy work, I came across three common reasons why marketers did not test their drafts:

- I didn't think of it
- I didn't have the time
- I didn't have the money.

Avoid these three traps and please:

- think of it
- take the time
- spend the money.

Look at your company culture

Company Culture	
Do it right the first time	Test and adjust
Zero failure tolerance	Accept failures
Do a perfect job	Try it out
Total Quality Management	Learn by trial and error

Some company cultures do not encourage testing.

Indicative of such a risk-averse culture are admonishments such as 'Do it right the first time', 'Do a perfect job', 'No mistakes allowed'. These statements do have their justification in production and quality control, but stifle new approaches to marketing.

Only a 'Test and adjust' or 'Try and learn' attitude in a blame-free company culture will encourage people to find innovative solutions to problems.

Move to the flagship phase

The Flagship Phase

Once your **Message Words Style Layout Diagrams Images** have been found clear and convincing by your customers

You can move from the 'submarine' (pre-launch) phase to the flagship phase once you have developed a persuasive package with a compelling story.

How will you know that you have achieved this objective?

Once the test results show that your clients feel that your words, style, layout, diagrams and images are clear and convincing.

Kick-start the roll-out

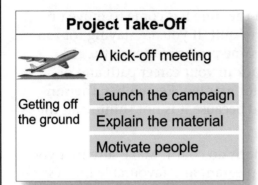

Organize a 'kick-off meeting'. Make this a highly visible official event and use the opportunity to:

- launch the campaign and highlight the objectives
- explain the promotional material
- show people what is in it for them.

In addition, you can collect information; for example the contact details of all team members.

Why not suggest some rules? For example: Let's use the expression 'Examplex ABC' to open the subject line of all emails. This will help us recognize and sort emails by project. Thus this procedure will facilitate finding key information.

Move into selling mode

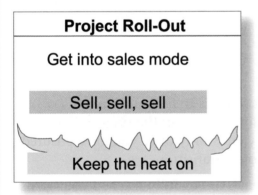

During the implementation phase you should be in sales mode.

Hit high gear. Your motto is 'sell'.

Don't bear grudges. Sceptics who have been doubting and questioning the value of your project suddenly show interest. What do you do? Forgive them. Forget the past. Get over their previous resistance and welcome them to the team.

Remember: 'On board is on board'.

Plan your exit strategy

Notice when the time has come to move on. Know when to quit. If you are staying for too long on the same project, you run the risk of getting stuck in your career path and of being taken for granted. Remember: the sun is appreciated because it is not shining all the time.

Last impressions do count. Make sure that your exit leaves a pleasant and favourable impression. Learn the art of closing.

Remember: there is a time for each and every thing.

The first option is for you to bring the project to a seemingly natural close.

In which case it's up to you to declare when you have accomplished your mission.

You have successfully reached your goals.

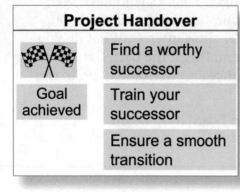

The second option is to find and train a good successor. Hand over the project. Your responsibility ends only once you have ensured a smooth project transition.

Again, you have successfully reached your goals.

Celebrate your team's achievements

Celebration

Relax and enjoy

Relish success

Take pleasure in your accomplishments

Winning is fun

Jack Welch

Party time: Celebrate the team's achievements

Once your time on the project is successfully concluded, it is time to celebrate.

Loosen up and relax. It's leisure time.

Organize a party and have a good time.

Relish your team's success.

Learn to derive pleasure from your accomplishments.

Enjoy the fruits of your work.

Depart with style

Your Departure

Thank everybody

Finishing power

Leave quickly

Move on to the next project

Thank everyone involved.

Depart from the project team with style - quickly and graciously.

Then move on to your next project.

Resist the temptation to hang around the project. This may be a painful and difficult decision, but it is important to make the break. Be firm.

IMPLEMENTING THE PROJECT

Success is based on strategies actually enacted, plans actually realized, projects actually executed. In order to finish what you have started, you need to adapt your mindset from 'thinker and planner' to 'mover and shaker'. This section shows you how.

Make a difference

Effective Implementation
Be known for
Delivering results
Achieving objectives
Successfully executing projects
She makes things happen	He gets things done

Your goal is to be known for:

- achieving lasting results and long-term effects
- accomplishing your strategic objectives
- successfully executing projects in the face of resistance.

This implies physically moving and doing things that move the project forward towards completion. This a skill that can be learned. Learn to do it even more effectively than you are doing it now.

Develop your storyboard

Examplex: The Movie

Film script .... You

Director .... You

Producer .... Your company

Lead players .... You, your colleagues, opinion leaders, etc.

Supporting cast .. Consultants, Journalists

Think of the trial results as the basis for a movie. You start by developing a concept on how the story will unfold. You write the film script. You are also the director who guides and coaches the actors.

Your company is the producer providing the money. The lead players are you, your colleagues, opinion leaders, and so on. The supporting cast is made up of consultants, journalists, agency people and others.

Keep timelines

Keep Timelines

Timing is everything

Motto of the Gatwick Express

Project activities must follow a certain schedule

'Timing is everything.' That is the motto of the 'Gatwick Express', the train running between Gatwick Airport and Victoria Railway Station in London. Make it also your credo. It is essential that the activities of your action plan are implemented on time.

Some software companies offer sophisticated project management support software packages. You may use them to produce detailed plans and nice flow charts on your computer screen and on paper. I personally never needed them. Remember, it's always people who get the job done.

Make the right things happen at the right time

The sequence of events is essential. You need to make sure that the right things happen at the right time. Plan your activities in the logical order.

Just as you have to add ingredients like sugar, flour and water in the right sequence in order to bake a cake, you need to plan the proper schedule of events in order to market clinical trial results successfully. Otherwise you will end up with a mess.

Start with the action plan

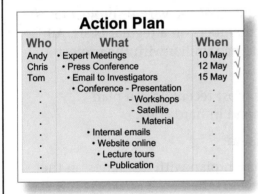

Develop a logical, coherent and consistent action plan. This plan should organize the work flow. Make it short; one or two pages at the most. Long action plans usually never get implemented. Set realistic deadlines. Observe the sequence of events. Make sure you specify who will do what and by when.

Develop the plan with your team. Ask team members what they think are reasonable deadlines. You are looking for their buy-in. If you can accommodate the dates they suggest in your overall project schedule, do so. Otherwise explain why an earlier deadline is needed.

If you have a formal 'Marketing Plan', 'Product Strategy Plan' or 'Commercialisation Plan', add the project action plan to this.

Communicate your deadlines

Deadline	
The **latest** time by which something must be completed	Get things done: Set realistic deadlines Communicate the dates

A deadline is the latest date by which some task must be completed.

You won't get things done until you set a deadline.

You need to communicate the importance of your deadlines very distinctly to all involved.

Make it clear that you take deadlines seriously.

Update your action plan

Making Timelines Visible	
Update action plans regularly	
	Electronically by email
	Physically with a printed version

Share the deadlines of the various project tasks with all team members on a regular basis. All of them should be familiar with the project schedule.

Distribute the most recent action plan electronically and in hard copy.

Electronic version:

- post the action plan with deadlines on the intranet
- send regular reminder emails to team members.

Hard copy version:

- produce a printed version and distribute it regularly to team members
- post a printed version on one of the walls of your office
- remember: deadlines printed in black and white have more impact than those displayed electronically on a computer screen.

Keep the project moving forward

Monitoring Performance

Follow up — Assess progress to see if deadlines are met

Check adherence to timelines

Verify if milestones are reached

Continuously assess the progress of your project. Ensure regular follow-up. Remember: what gets measured, gets done.

One senior executive once asked the clinical project manager 'How did this project get ten weeks behind schedule?' The answer 'One day at a time'. Work on your project every day.

Do not postpone, delay, put off or defer timelines, unless absolutely necessary.

Do not prevaricate.

Conduct regular review meetings

Regular Project Reviews

Routine Review — Schedule a rhythm of meetings, for example every Monday morning

Are we on schedule?   Is our project on track?

You need to schedule and hold regular review meetings. Establish a rhythm, so that people know in advance when their progress will be judged. For example, you might invite your team members to regular Monday morning meetings. During these meetings ask:

- are we on schedule?
- is our project on track?
- do we keep the course?
- do we observe the timelines?

If necessary, remind people of pending deadlines.

Find a project coordinator

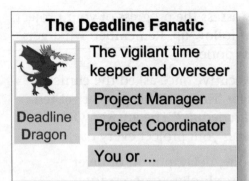

Who will invite team members to these regular review meetings? Who is the guardian of the project time lines? You need a project coordinator, someone who assumes the role of 'chief scheduler' and who diligently tracks project progress from day to day. This coordinator checks whether people actually implement the plan on time. If not, he or she will remind people and help them to avoid procrastination. This is an important and demanding role.

The best people for this job are persons who are good completers or finishers, those with an edge for detail, who like to see things through. Do you wish to assume that role yourself? Or can you think of someone suitable in the team? Or do you wish to talk to your boss and your human resource department about a possible candidate?

Hold people accountable

Make sure you hold people accountable. Reward those who keep to deadlines. Give them credit. Show that you care and that you appreciate their reliability. Recognize their efforts towards achieving a common goal.

Do not tolerate people who frequently overrun their deadlines. Admonish them. You may not have formal authority over team members who miss their deadlines. So you need to sit down with them.

Emphasize that time discipline is essential to the team's success. Point out the consequences of the overrun and explain why this might jeopardize the overall project success. Try to find a solution. If the two of you cannot work out a way forward, initiate a joint conversation with that person's boss.

Make sure everything is on time

The Timing Speed Example

How quickly were slides of results available following the first official presentation?

☐ within 1 month
☐ within 1 week
☒ on the same day

Company representatives handed out the slides immediately after the session.

Opportunity well used!

Have a look at the example and think what you and your team would be able to achieve. If you mark any option other than 'on the same day' you may wish to think about how to improve your project management.

Timing is everything when it comes to communication campaigns for clinical trial results. So make sure everything and everybody is on time!

Avoid missing opportunities

The Timing Delay Example

N trial results: **D** significantly reduced stroke. After the presentation at a major congress, company representatives at the booth offered

☐ CD-ROM with study results
☐ Brochure with study results
☐ An abstract on a sheet of paper
☒ Nice coffee mugs

Missed Opportunity

In this real-life example, the results of a trial were very positive: the substance 'D' reduced the stroke risk significantly. The principal investigator presented these encouraging results at a major European congress. Many people (including myself) showed up at the company booth in the industry exhibition and asked for details. All the company representatives could offer were nice coffee mugs. Clearly a missed huge opportunity!

Think about what supporting material your team can offer at your company booth immediately after the first official presentation. Will you get everything ready to present a CD-ROM or a brochure or at least an abstract?

BECOMING A PROJECT LEADER

Even if you are not formally leading the parade, you can assume intellectual and social leadership for a project which will turn you into the 'de facto' project leader.

Remember the key success factor

People As Success Factor

People come first

Top-flight talent on board?

It's people who make it or break it

The three key success factors according to Don Petersen (successful Ford executive and corporate philosopher) are: people, products and profit - in that order.

Remember:

- people are the lifeblood of the project
- people are the heart of the project.

Some managers, however, pay only lip service to these statements and wonder why their projects fail or their businesses flounder.

Can you make these statements come to life in your own small group or team?

See what you can do to make it real.

Build a winning team

A Winning Team

Get the best people to help you

Game of Business

Sir Richard Branson
Founder of Virgin Group

Usually the team with the best players wins

Learn to recognize people who are good at what they do. Learn to identify people with potential. Luckily, great people are everywhere. You should be looking for them among various groups (peers, assistants, students, junior people, support staff) and in various places within your company (marketing, market research, clinical development). Look for people with talent. Try to get the best people on board.

You may not be able to hire these people formally or to win them over for the current project, but your contacts may prove valuable for your next project. In the long run, try to surround yourself with people who are smarter and better than you are. Do not leave this important task to Human Resources.

Remember: if you have the wrong people in your team, then no strategy – no matter how brilliant it may be – will save you!

Make your project appealing

Attracting People

I would like to be on your team!

Make your project so appealing that people want to be part of it!

What would it take to make people sign up?

Bright volunteer who wants to join

You will only rarely have the opportunity to hire new people for your project. However you can attract people by making the project so attractive that it pulls people into your team.

People who hear about your project want to join your team. Make your project so interesting, innovative and instructive, that people will sign on and spend more hours per week on your project than on other (less interesting) projects.

Ideally people compete with each other for the privilege of being a member of your team.

Foster a great team culture

Good Team Culture	
Jointly performing a great project	Your team: A vital, vibrant and dynamic place where people
	Take risks
	Learn
	Grow

Think about how to create an exciting team spirit so people feel drawn to your team. Your team should be a place where people can learn new stuff, where they can try new things, where they can grow, where there is fun and excitement.

Team members should enjoy working with you on the project.

Remember: happy teams have an easier time winning than unhappy teams.

Become the 'de facto' project leader

Project Leadership	
Guiding others	Show initiative
	Take on challenges
	Convey a sense of meaning
	Become a great person to work with

Lead from within. Show initiative. Show that you like to take on the challenges the team's project offers. Show that you love to work on the project.

Convey a sense of direction and purpose to the project. Guide and motivate your team members. Inspire people by your presence.

Create an environment in which their creativity will thrive. Leadership today involves acting more as coach rather than as supervisor.

Engender trust and credibility

Trust and Credibility

Be authentic

Be candid

Admit mistakes

Keep your promises

Integrity: Accept responsibility for your actions

People are drawn to those who display trustworthiness and integrity. Lead by example.

- Be credible. Be sincere. Be authentic. Be real
- If there are setbacks, admit your mistakes. Do not try to cover up your failures. Avoid blaming others if things go wrong. After all, you are human and not perfect
- Fulfil your promises. Keep your word, so make sure you underpromise and overdeliver.

Show stature and take responsibility for your decisions and actions. Walk the talk.

Exude optimism

Positive Attitude

Up-beat wins

Be confident

Show drive

Exude optimism

Emanate enthusiasm

We can do it

Your state of mind will influence everyone in the team.

Be pragmatic and display a positive attitude:

- be confident even when meeting resistance
- show drive and initiative in overcoming obstacles
- pour out optimism and give positive energy to the team
- communicate your enthusiasm or even your passion for the project.

Relish change.

Offer benefits to your team

Personal Aspirations

What's the advantage for me?

What's in it for me?

What people really want

Which benefits can you offer?

Your team members are looking for what they can gain if they commit themselves fully to your project. Take time to explore their aspirations and communicate the benefits of participating in the team.

You cannot command commitment. People will commit themselves to the project only if you can convince them that it is of benefit to them.

Show that you care deeply for your colleagues and for the project.

Train your team

Learning Opportunity

Offer great training

Develop a curriculum of topics

Organize educational workshops

Provide cutting-edge information

Personal and professional growth

Develop a curriculum of topics for training your team members. Add a strong educational aspect to all your workshops. Invite an in-house expert, an opinion leader or an internal or external marketing trainer who can update their know-how. Teach them, but do not pontificate. Provide cutting-edge information for your team members.

Make it clear that being a member of your team is a great learning opportunity. You provide access to exciting tasks. This will make it easier for you to attract the people you want on your projects.

Remember: developing and nurturing people is a daily task. Use every opportunity to advise and coach your team members.

Provide a professional experience

A Professional Experience

Attractive site

Discovery

Adventure

Excitement

We are writing product history

Keep people interested

You can create a sense of excitement by using themes and statements that catch the imagination and arouse curiosity. Some of the topics on the example may work well.

People perform better when they are in a vital setting. Add an element of surprise and suspense. Your team is alive and vibrant with energy.

Think about the location for your product manager or marketing and sales workshop and, if you can afford it, choose somewhere stimulating and attractive. Think of additional ways to keep people interested in your project.

Motivate your team

Motivation

Keep up the morale

Encourage people

Energize your team

Do not demotivate people

Keep up the momentum

Remember: motivation is the motif for action. Marketing and Motivation go hand-in-glove. It is your responsibility to keep up the morale. Make people act at a higher level by keeping them highly motivated!

Your company maybe undergoing a restructure. Perhaps people in the organization are demotivated and don't enjoy their workplace. You can create an oasis. You need to be a great person to work with, on a great project, with a great team. Energize your team. Keep up the momentum in the group.

Demand performance

Performance	
	Tap all inner sources
	Demand contributions
Challenge	Request great work
Push yourself and your team members to new heights	

Demand performance (not perfection) from your team members.

Challenge them:

- appeal to their commitment to action
- demand their important contributions
- request the great work they are capable of.

Ask them to deliver results.

Push yourself and your team members to new heights.

Take time to praise people

Praise and Recognition	
Super!	Praise
	Acclaim
	Compliments
	Congratulations
Energize people	The more specific, the better

Take time to praise people associated with the project when they have done a great job. Successful marketers are great enthusiasts, lavish with their praise.

Prescribe yourself a course in recognizing special efforts.

Recognize your team members' and even your boss's special efforts.

Create an atmosphere of recognition in your team.

Give compliments; the more specific, the better.

Build self-confidence in your team members

Building Confidence	
 Prize	Show respect
	Extend thanks
	Give appreciation
	Share rewards

Inject confidence into your team.

It is the fuel for teams that win.

Give your team members a feeling of importance because they are important.

Give the people in your team what everybody wants:
respect, attention, appreciation.

Make them feel special.

Write their birthday dates into your calendar and celebrate the day.

Good leaders show that they really care about their people.

Give your team members the credit they deserve.

Share the rewards.

Offer empathy

Team Empathy
Make your team members feel part of the 'family'
Companionship and a sense of camaraderie

Make your team members feel part of the 'family'. Give them a sense of belonging. If you feel uncomfortable with the word 'family', choose your own vocabulary (group, team, crew). Terms such as this are preferable to more anonymous terms such as department, business unit, or company.

Make your team members feel that they really are your colleagues, your associates, your partners and your fellow professionals.

Keep your people

Retention Strategy
Mentor the individual
Support their careers
Initiate 'apprenticeships'
People leave managers, not companies

How do you keep the bright people in your team once they have joined it? How do you retain brilliant people? How do you make them stay with the project?

- become their mentor and adviser
- support their ambitions. Foster their careers
- if you have a junior person or assistant in the team, look at the possibility of some kind of apprenticeship.

Create opportunities for them. Split your project into subprojects or tasks. Encourage team members to regard these tasks as personal development opportunities.

Nurturing people's growth is not something that you do when there is time left over in your schedule. Devote time to this important task. It will pay off in the long run.

ACTION

Be awake

Waking Up	
	**Be alert**
A new morning	**Act**
Make every day count	

Benefit from the opportunities the day offers you.

Make every day a special day for you.

Pay attention to the moment.

Be present.

Be alert.

Act.

Live up to your potential

Rising to New Heights	
	No one can predict to what heights you can soar
Even you will not know until you spread your wings	

It is your life.

You decide.

Enter the great game.

The Hopi Indians in North America say about your true potential in life that 'No one can predict to what heights you can soar.

Even you will not know until you spread your wings.'

Spread your wings!

SUGGESTED FURTHER READING

Moi Ali, Stephen Brookson, Andy Bruce, John Eaton, Robert Heller, Roy Johnson, Ken Langdon, Steve Sleight (2002), *Managing for Excellence* (Dorling Kindersley).

Laura Brown and Tony Grundy (2004), *Project Management for the Pharmaceutical Industry* (Gower).

David Currier with Jay Frost (2001), *Be brief. Be bright. Be gone. Career Essentials for Pharmaceutical Representatives* (Universe Inc Book Publisher).

Reiner Czichos (2002), *Change Management* (Ernst Reinhardt Verlag).

Erwin Dichtl, Hans Raffée, Michael Thiess (1989), *Innovatives Pharma-Marketing* (Gabler Verlag, Wiesbaden).

Dolores M. Frías (2000), *Marketing farmacéutico* (Ediciones Pirámide (Group Anaya)).

Harald Friesewinkel (1992), *Pharma-Business* (E. Habrich Verlag, Berlin).

Ford Harding (1994), *Rain making. The Professional's Guide to Attracting New Clients* (Bob Adams, Inc., An F+W Publications Company).

Philip Kotler (1999), *Kotler on Management: How to create, win and dominate markets* (The Free Press, Simon & Schuster).

John Lidstone (2003), *Presentation Planning and Media Relations for the Pharmaceutical Industry* (Gower).

Michael Lonsert and Klaus-Jürgen Preuß & Eckhard Kucher (1995), *Handbuch Pharma-Management* (Gabler Verlag, Wiesbaden).

Janice MacLennan (2004), *Brand Planning for the Pharmaceutical Industry* (Gower).

David H. Maister (2000), *True Professionalism - The courage to care about your people, your clients, and your career* (Free Press).

Albert Mehrabian (1981), *Silent messages: Implicit communication of emotions and attitudes* (Wadsworth).

Franz Metcalf, BJ Callagher (2001), *What would Buddha do at work?* (Seastone, an imprint of Ulysses Press).

Robert B Miller, Stephen E Heiman (1987), *Conceptual Selling* (Miller-Heimann, Inc).

David Ogilvy (1983), *Ogilvy on Advertising* (New York, Crown).

Tom Peters (1999), *The Professional Service Firm 50*; *The Brand You 50*; *The Project 50* (Series published by Alfred A. Knopf, Inc. Copyright 1999 by Excel/A California).

Tom Peters (2003), *Re-Imagine* (Dorling Kindersley Limited).

B. Joseph Pine II and James H. Gilmore (2000), *The Experience Economy – Work is Theatre and Every Business a Stage* (Two audiocassettes, HighBridge Company, St. Paul, Minnesota, USA).

Ben Renshaw (2000), *Successful but something is missing: Daring to enjoy life to the full* (Published by Rider).

Al Ries and Laura Ries (1998), *The 22 Immutable Laws of Branding* (HarperCollins Publishers).

William Strunk Jr & EB White (2002), *The Elements of Style* (Allyn & Bacon. A Pearson Education Company).

Thomas Trilling (2003), *Pharma-Marketing* (Springer).

Peter Mc Williams (1995), *You cannot afford the luxury of a negative thought* (The Life 101 Series, Prelude Press, Inc).

ABOUT THE AUTHOR

Dr Günter Umbach is a board-certified gynaecologist, with experience as an oncology research fellow at the University of Texas, USA. Subsequently, he became product manager and then marketing director in a global research-based pharmaceutical company. He also worked as a medical director in a generics firm.

As a corporate manager, he assumed responsibility for marketing the clinical trial results of a billion-euro brand. As international brand team leader he developed in-house workshops to train his marketing colleagues how to effectively convert scientific data into prescription incentives. His team achieved the highest sales in the history of the product.

He now manages *Healthcare Marketing Dr Umbach & Partner*, a marketing services firm which specializes in training, advising and coaching marketing professionals in the healthcare sector. He gives advanced seminars in cities throughout Europe.

His clients benefit from his more than 25 years' experience in the healthcare market as prescribing physician, as marketer in the pharmaceutical industry, and as trainer and consultant.

He is a faculty member at a European management school, a lecturer at two German business-oriented universities, the instructor of the Forum Pharma Marketing Diploma course and an author on continuing marketing education. He is also a member of the Professional Expert Groups Business Coaching and Consultants of the American National Speakers Association.

Contact him at www.umbachpartner.com